George de Vallière

Opals from a Mexican Mine

George de Vallière

Opals from a Mexican Mine

ISBN/EAN: 9783743303737

Manufactured in Europe, USA, Canada, Australia, Japa

Cover: Foto ©Thomas Meinert / pixelio.de

Manufactured and distributed by brebook publishing software
(www.brebook.com)

George de Vallière

Opals from a Mexican Mine

OPALS

FROM A MEXICAN MINE

BY

GEORGE DE VALLIÈRE

NEW AMSTERDAM BOOK COMPANY ❧ ❧
PUBLISHERS ❧ ❧ NEW YORK ❧ ❧ MDCCCXCVI

" Now, opals are the tears shed by Tonatiuh, the Sun God, many ages ago, and which fell upon the earth and have lodged in its bosom, turning into jewels. It was prophesied by our forefathers that men would labor wearily for them and kings would pay great price of gold therefor. Hence it is well to know the virtues and portents of these stones, and may wise men ponder deeply upon what I, Chimapopotl, a descendant of the high priest, will say. Now, some [of these stones] are white, though veined with red when held to the light, and these portend love and death . . . and there are some that shimmer with the blue of Heaven, and these speak of love . . . passion rings loud in those that are of the hue of gold. . . . If a man take into his hand one that is yellow changing into cloud-like gray, and sleep, he will have strange dreams . . . and it is also true that one may find a handful of divers hues which may mean anything or nothing, as one will."—*Extract from an ancient Nahuatl manuscript in Queretaro.*

CONTENTS

The Greatest of the Gods is Quetzalcoatl

" And some are white, though veined
with red when held to the light,
and these portend love and death."

The Greatest
of the
Gods
is
Quetzalcoatl

TEZCOMAYA is builded in the hollow of a
plain, wherein it differs not from most
towns in the Republic of Mexico. All about this
plain the Sierra strikes its purple teeth into the
sky of everlasting blue, these deepening into
black when they meet the stars at nightfall. Far
to the east lies the valley plain of Anahuac, and
to the west the mountains slope down to the sea
till the sands are washed by the lazy surges of
the Pacific.

A cluster of adobe houses huddled around a
dusty plazuela, and then straggling out into a
single street that ends in brushwood huts, and

finally sprawls into the desert ; here and there a tree that sulks and is ashamed ; a small church with galleried campanile, wherein hang bells that softly ring the hours of sleep and prayer ; dust, dogs, and donkeys—such is Tezcomaya.

The people toil not, nor spin, nor are they well clothed. Meekly they bear the burden of life, aided thereto by a long draught of mezcal now and then, whereupon they sleep, and per- haps dream. A league away is a hole in the ground, a mine denounced and mastered by men from the North, and here some of the na- tives move with pretence of labor, though still dreaming.

One October day, in the year of our Lord 1892, Tonatiuh rose, as he had done since the last universal cataclysm, in a sky of unflecked blue, seemingly indifferent that he was not met, as of yore, with greeting songs and garlanded dance. Well here, as elsewhere, had the cowled head done its work, and only the surpliced priest in the adobe church bowed and genuflexed before images of gaudy hue, all of which had nothing to do with the old god.

Just as the bright beams tipped the eastern Sierra, a girl darted out from one of the adobe houses, passed the door of the church without even the sign of the cross, despite the tinkling of the bell within, and hurried away to the north. She was clothed in a plain sleeveless garment of cotton cloth, and her face, all but her dark eyes, was hidden under a heavy rebozo of black thread, whose fine and delicate weft cost many a day of ceaseless toil, and stamped the wearer as wealthier than her fellows.

The girl's bare feet left a clear imprint upon the soft white dust of the plazuela and of the street as she sped swiftly along, past the last straggling huts of Tezcomaya, and out upon the smooth cactus-flecked plain that levelled away to the foot of the Sierra rising like a boundary wall a good six leagues away. Mile after mile she passed at a seemingly tireless gait that was more a run than a walk, though her throat and nostrils were parched and choked with the fine powder of the desert, and her feet torn to bleeding by the spines of the cactus.

The earth glowed like a furnace under the fierce heat of the sun, and the girl panted like a hunted deer, her dry tongue licking her lips, but never once did she relax her speed. Soon the Sierra grew more distinct, its buttresses, battlements, towers, and ravines marked themselves out of the purple mist. Not a tree nor a bush grew upon the shrivelled slopes, not a bird hovered in the air above ; it was the desolation of heat, not death, for here life had never been. Columns of dust marched like giant spectres across the plain which swept off here and there into mirage lakes that shimmered with light.

Straight toward the wall of rock the girl ran, as if to hurl herself against it; but when she could almost touch it with her hand, there appeared a narrow cleft, and into this she entered. Here she was in the cool shadow, for this was the domain of Mictlantecutli, into which Tonatiuh could never come. Scarce was she within when she sat, or rather fell, upon the rocky floor and bowed down until her forehead touched the cold stone, her breath coming quick and short, her limbs trembling. Thus she remained for some moments until the heaving of her full rounded breasts grew less rapid, and then, as if with new strength, she leapt to her feet and pursued her way through the narrow gorge, now climbing over huge boulders that blocked the path, now leaping across black holes that yawned beneath her feet, yet always surely, as one who knows the way well, difficult though it is.

As she advanced, the walls of the gorge leaned together and met above, shutting out the light of day. She plunged fearlessly on, though with slower step, for in the thick darkness hands took the place of eyes, reaching and feeling for the sides of the narrow tunnel. Her foot touched something soft and cold, and she drew it up quickly with a low cry. She stood motionless as an image of stone, and called with half-voice :

"Nantli Colotl!"

She craned her neck, listening. Her voice seemed to travel a long way and then come back to her in a faint echo : "Colotl." Again she called, this time loudly, straining her throat to its utmost of sound : "Nantli Colotl!" Another sound now thrilled to her in the blackness : "Nelli, nelli, teichpoch!"

The girl breathed a sigh of relief as she answered in the Nahuatl tongue : "Yes, it is I, your daughter, Xicaltetecon. I wish to see you quickly, but dare not come farther, for the way is full of your children, the cohuatl."

A low soft hiss breathed down the tunnel, and the girl could feel, rather than hear, the gliding of the sinuous bodies of the snakes on the rocky floor, as they answered the call of their mistress. She stepped forward slowly, putting her foot down with care, lest it touch one of the reptiles whom she knew were moving on ahead of her. She went but a short distance, and then, turning sharply to the left, emerged from the narrow way

into a great cavern which was brilliant with the
flames of a fire that leapt and curled upon a huge
stone altar. Near this, her hand resting upon it,
stood a tall bronzed woman, clad only in a sash
of bright yellow wrapt closely about her hips and
knotted in front. She was not old, for not a
single wrinkle marred her regular features, and
her dark eyes glowed with strength and passion ;
nor young, for her face had something of the
majesty that comes from knowledge born of
long experience. On her wrists and ankles were
heavy bands of gold, and strips of the same
metal glittered, interwoven, in the long hair that
fell to her knees, covering her as with a mantle
of jet. About her neck was a thin chain of silver
that held suspended between her breasts a golden
image of the sun, the centre and rays of which
seemed to glow with a light of their own.

Such was Nantli Colotl (Mother Scorpion), the
far famed Bruja de los Montes, or witch of the
mountains, in whose existence the Spaniard
denied a belief, though he spoke of her reluc-

2

tantly and with some fear beneath. They—
the immaterial and undefinable "they"—said
that there lived in the Sierra a priestess of the old
cult, and that some of the Indios went thither to
worship; but the padre, a stern man, proclaimed
this a lie of Satan himself, and dangerous to the
soul's future even to think about. Xicaltetecon
walked up to the priestess, and, holding out her
hands appealingly, fell upon her knees.

"Well, girl," said the woman, looking coldly
at the form at her feet, "'tis a long time since
thy butterfly wings have brought thee hither,
and I think thou wouldst never have come again
had not——"

"Pity, Nantli Colotl !" pleaded the girl in the
soft Nahuatl tongue ; "I will tell thee——"

"Tell *me !*" exclaimed the priestess scornfully,
"thou wilt tell *me* something ! Nay, I will tell
thee what thou camest for. Thy lover, the
golden-haired stranger from the North, lies ill,
ill of the fever that the Spaniard cannot cure, the
curse of Mictlantecutli, and on the seventh day

he will die, and thou wouldst beg me to save him. Do I speak the truth of Quetzalcoatl?"

The breasts of the girl heaved quickly and her voice quivered with pain. "Yes, Nantli, it is true. Thou knowest all things. Thou wilt save him, save him, Nantli, for my father's sake!"

"Thou darest mention thy father's name!" exclaimed the priestess angrily; "what hast thou in common with him? He served our god here till the Spanish priest caused him to be thrown into a dungeon, where he died. Thou didst flit away to live with the Spaniards, and almost hast thou gone into their church and bowed down to their maquechitli (dolls), and thou speakest their tongue as glibly as if thou wert a chattering monototl (parrot) thyself."

"Nay, nay, Nantli," sobbed the girl; "never have I been false to my father's teachings; never have I entered the door of the house of the singing priest, nor bowed to the velvet-robed virgin. My lover is not one of the Spaniards whom thou hatest.   Thou wilt save him, Nantli ?   I will die if he die ! "

"Ca, ca.   Thou speakest of dying like a Spaniard, as if it were some great thing."   The priestess stopped and placed both of her hands over her eyes.   After a moment's pause she continued in a low and hesitating voice, as of one speaking with great difficulty, "Yes, I see thee dead, and thy lover with the gold hair standing with a foot upon thy grave.   It is so written."

The girl rose to her feet, and with the fringe of her rebozo wiped away the tears that stained her brown cheeks.

"Then let it be so, Nantli.   If thou dost wish my life for his it is thine.   It was not death I feared, but leaving him."

"I have naught to do with thy life, Xicaltetecon," said the priestess, taking down her hands and seeming to recover herself.   "That is in the hands of the dark forms who stand behind Quetzalcoatl, and whose messenger he is.   I told thee what I saw, nothing more."

"A prophecy?" murmured the girl. "Those of our people have not always come true. My father taught me to read the signs upon those walls," and she pointed with her finger to some hieroglyphics that were deeply cut upon one of the sides of the cavern. "That says, and it was so spoken by Guatemozin, that at this time our people shall again rule the land. Yet it is not so!"

The priestess looked at Xicaltetecon with an expression of contempt. "Thou art but half learned in our mysteries, and of facts thou knowest no more than thy namesake which flits from flower to flower. Dost thou not know that he whose throne is in the ancient city, and who rules with iron hand to-day our land from the river of the North to where the oceans eat into the earth until they are but a span apart, is one of our own people, with not a drop of Spanish blood in his veins? Does not Diaz descend straight from our prince Guatemozin, and is not the prophecy thus fulfilled?"

The girl bowed her head. "Thou art right. Speak, I will do whatsoever thou tellest me."

For a while the priestess did not answer. The light upon the great stone table had grown dim. Nantli Colotl picked up from the floor what appeared to be a piece of yellow stone and threw it upon the smoldering fire. It crackled fiercely, and long curling tongues of flame shot up that illumined the farthest recesses of the cavern. At this something upon the altar moved—something that looked at first like a heap of feathers—and coiled itself into a snake, lifting its head and darting out its forked tongue toward the priestess.

"Down, Mitzli !" she commanded ; and then turning to the girl, who had shrunk back at the sight of the feathered monster, "Why art thou afraid of Mitzli ? It is through him that Quetzalcoatl speaks, the greatest of all the gods, he who taught our people and guides them to-day, if they would but listen !" As she reverently spoke the name of the mysterious god she pointed to a face sculptured in the rock on one side of the cavern—the sad, pleading face of a man, wise in the wisdom that is born of suffering ; the same face that struck awe to the heart of the invading, Christ-worshipping Spaniard when he found it upon the ruins of ancient temples, so like was it to that of his own thorn-filleted God.

The priestess dropped her hand to her side and stood for a moment in deep thought ; then, a cruel light flashing in her eyes, she looked at the girl, who stood with clasped hands, mutely awaiting the decision.

"I am not all powerful, Xicaltetecon, that thou knowest. This much can I do for thee if thou wilt obey me, no more. Swear by the face of Quetzalcoatl, by thy father's spirit which now stands beside thee, that thou wilt obey me if I cure thy lover, no matter what it is I ask."

"I swear it !" cried the girl, holding out her hands to the sculptured face that looked pityingly down upon her.

"Good ! Now listen. To-night, ere the

moon rise, I will come to the choza where thou
livest with thy lover, and I will apply to him the
cure known to us.   If at the end of three hours
the fever die out and he be as those are who get
well, thou shalt leave him and go to the choza of
José, the arriero, who is one of us, and who has
loved thee long and faithfully, and thou shalst
live with him."

The girl staggered back and the muscles of her
face contracted.   "Never ! Death if thou wilst,—
I agree to that—but not life with José while my
lover lives !   Never, never !"   The last word
was a moan ending in a sob.

The priestess shrugged her shoulders impatiently.   "I have said it.   Only upon that condition will I save the man from the North.   You
may choose."

With a cry of agony the girl fell upon her
knees and again held out her hands imploringly
to the sorrowful god.

"Help !" she cried ; "Quetzalcoatl ! Spirit of
my father, help !"

As the last word was spoken there seemed to come whisperings as if from the walls, and a low moan shuddered through the cavern and died away. There was the sound as of the light treading of many feet upon the stone floor, but Xicaltetecon could see nothing, only a great tremor shook her from head to foot, pricking her as with needles lightly touched upon the skin. The feathered snake writhed as if it had been impaled, and the flames that arose from the burning stone shot horizontally along the surface of the altar, hissing as if a strong wind had blown upon them. Purple lights flashed in the shadowy dome above, like the gleams of swinging scimeters, and for an instant the earth rocked beneath the feet of the priestess and her victim. Gradually the sounds died away, the snake grew motionless and coiled again into a bunch of feathers. All was as it had been before the cry of the girl stirred the shadowy things that are behind the veil.

The expression of surprise, not unmingled with

fear, which had shown itself upon the face of the priestess at the first manifestation of the powers she served, now gave place to one of triumph.

" As I thought ! " she exclaimed ; " it is written, and they could not change it if they would."

The girl made a last effort to bend her foe. She looked fixedly at the priestess, her eyes flashing with magnetic force.

"Listen, Nantli," she said ; " if I cannot change the fates, thou canst, for this thing of José, the arriero, is thy will, not theirs. Give me a little time with my lover after he is cured, to see once more the love-light in his eyes, to feel once more his kisses upon my lips, to bid him farewell when he can know me ; for now the fever has changed his soul and he knows nothing. Only a month, Nantli—a week—a few little days ! "

Again the priestess shook her head and the evil light flashed in her sensuous eyes.

" It is useless, Xicaltetecon. If I sell, thou must pay the price I demand. But decide quickly," she added, with an impatient stamp of her foot that made the golden anklets ring. "At the falling of the sun some come here to worship ; the way is far from here to Tezcomaya, and there is much to do for this thing."

The girl crossed her hands upon her breast and bowed her head with the fatalism inherited from her forefathers, who had mounted with firm step the teocalli and given their hearts to the sun-god.

"I will do as thou wishest," she said, in a quiet, firm voice.

The priestess fixed her eyes upon those of Xicaltetecon. "Thou art weary," she said ; "thou must rest ere thou goest back, or thou wilt fall by the wayside. Sleep !"

The sharp command caused the girl to start, but she could not take her eyes from those of the priestess, which had become two centres of circles of flowing, dazzling light. The lids of Xicaltetecon closed, and she would have fallen had not her companion caught her. Nantli Colotl bore the limp body across the cavern and laid it upon a heap of jaguar skins.

She stood over the girl for a moment, contemplating the exquisite Madonna-like face which in the hypnotic slumber looked drawn and infinitely sad.   She bent down and put her fingers upon the sleeper's forehead.   "Dream," she commanded ; "dream of thy lover !"   The muscles of the girl's face relaxed into a smile, her breathing became almost imperceptible.

The priestess now turned to the stone altar and took from beneath it a jar of baked clay with narrow curved neck.   Into this she poured liquid from another jar and pushed in a handful of dried leaves and some white powder.   She placed the vessel upon the flames and stood watching it until a light cloud of steam curled up from it. She then removed the jar, and, holding it by the neck, whirled it rapidly around at arm's length that it might cool more quickly.   Replacing it upon the altar, beside the sleeping snake, she began a low droning chant in the Nahuatl, the original Aztec tongue, to the accompaniment of which she swayed her lithe body to and fro in the graceful rhythmic movements of a sensual dance, the one used of old when the sun was a passion god and the earth heaved toward him.

"Quetzalcoatl, Teuhtli, ca mochipa, ca nican nica. Te ticuati in notlanequiliz in motechcopa ! Macame ximomamatl in nohuicpa. Nictlazoca-mati ca nicuipcayotiz in cenca qualli nohuicpa oticchiuh. Cuix cualli."[1]

As the chant proceeded, the snake lifted its flat, triangular head, fixing its ruby eyes upon the woman, and then began to wave its head and the upper part of its body in exact imitation of her movements. It rose higher and higher until it stood upon a single coil of its tail, and when the dance ended, it stopped suddenly and re-mained as motionless as if carved in stone upon the walls of Xochicalco.

Slowly, her eyes fixed upon those of the mon-ster, the priestess approached until she was

---

[1] "Quetzalcoatl, always Lord, I am here. Thou knowest the worship I have for thee. Be not loth to give me what I ask. Thanks do I render, and I will compensate thee for the good thou hast done to me. It is good."

within arm's reach of it, and then, with a movement swifter than the eye could follow, seized it by the neck and thrust its head into the mouth of the jar. The snake twisted and writhed in fury, but the woman held firm for a few minutes, after which she released the snake and stepped quickly back, drawing away the jar.

"There, there, Mitzli," she murmured caressingly, "thou hast given me enough of thy venom. Tlein tiquelehuia, nehuatl mitzhualhuiquiliz, etzli acuetzapalin necuayotl." ("What wilt thou? I will bring it, lizard's blood and hydromel.") She put before the reptile a bowl into which it plunged its head greedily.

There was more of practical chemistry than magic in the priestess's preparation for the cure of the man who was dying of the fever. She tasted the mixture, and, seeming to find it good, put the jar aside and went over to where Xicaltetecon lay sleeping upon the jaguar skins. She leaned over and put her lips close to the girl's breast.

"When the bells in the Spanish priest's tower

strike three thou must go to the hut of José, the arriero. Now wake !"

At the last word she breathed upon the sleeper's eyelids. Xicaltetecon moved, drew up her arms, and opened her dark eyes.

"Have I slept long ?" she exclaimed, springing to her feet.

"Barely a half hour. The sun is not long upon the downward path. Drink from this cup."

The girl obeyed, taking a long draft of the sweet but powerful necuayotl, distilled from the honey of wild bees in the forests of the tierra caliente.

"To-night, then, when the moon rises, thou wilt come and bring the secret medicine ?" asked Xicaltetecon, handing back the cup.

"Nantli Colotl never failed to keep her promise," said the priestess, haughtily, "whether it were given for weal or woe. Let others look to theirs. Fare thee well, Xicaltetecon, and bear in mind to speak my name if thou meetest others coming here to worship, lest they kill thee as a spy."

"Nelli, nelli" ("It is well"), replied the girl, and turning, she hurried from the cave, threading cautiously but swiftly the dark passage, and was soon out upon the plain, under the hot rays of the sun.

The single-storied adobe house that had formerly belonged to the father of Xicaltetecon, known in Tezcomaya as Pedro Gutierrez, stood at the head of the street which, together with the plazuela, formed the town. The building was more pretentious than the others, more so even than that of the padre, by reason of its swinging wooden door, painted white, and its two windows with panes of glass guarded by heavy iron bars.

The interior, however, was but a single room, floored unevenly with reddish brick, which was covered here and there with bright-hued zarapes woven by the natives of Michoacan. A rough table, a few chairs and settee of bent wood, a huge chest of drawers, black and scarred, that had come from France in the days of Maximilian, and an iron bed, were all the furniture of which this room could boast. On the walls were prints and engravings cut from illustrated papers, some rifles and revolvers hanging from iron hooks. Through the half-open door that led into the little patio in the rear, one could see part of a brushwood shed, beneath which was the stone, cut at regular intervals with holes for the burning charcoal, and which served as a cooking-stove. Some lean chickens stalked about the sunburned yard, venturing now and then into the room, cautiously, and with quick, nervous twists of the head.

The room was deserted, save for some one who lay upon the bed, a form outlined under the white coverings. For a time it would lay quite still, and then, with a low moan, turn over, and two trembling, emaciated hands were stretched out as if in dumb pleading. As the form turned, a yellow, cadaverous face was exposed, covered with dark blotches that shaded from purple to brown. The eyes were closed in the stupor of the fever. An indescribable odor, peculiar to the typhus, filled the apartment.

The door opened, and a hag, wrinkled and bent with age, entered the room. Her face was so furrowed that no features were clearly distinguishable, save the hawk nose and the eyes that glittered like black crystals set in old mahogany. She saw the chickens which had wandered into the room, and drove them, with muttered curses, out into the patio, closing the door upon them. Then filling a clay cup from a jar that stood in the corner, she held it to the sick man's lips, crooning the while. The sufferer greedily drank the liquid and then sank back upon the hard pillow. The old woman replaced the cup, and after a glance to assure herself that the eyes of the sick man were closed, she put her hand down into the covers at the foot of the bed, and drew out a small leathern bag. This she opened, and peered greedily at the silver and copper coins within. Her long bony fingers picked out a tlaco, a copper coin worth but the fraction of a cent, and slipped it into a rent in the rag that served her as a dress. She carefully put back the bag, mumbling to herself, as if in justification of her petty theft : " Los muertos no pagan " (" The dead do not pay "), and then went out again, closing the street door softly behind her.

The shadows of the low houses grew longer, moving across the white dusty street till they clambered up the adobe fronts on the opposite side. The sun reddened as it dipped down to the Sierra, and a puff of chilling air swept in from the north. The bell in the church-tower toned the hour of vespers, and some charcoal burners, bent under the huge baskets they had carried that day from the wooded mountains which lay far to the west, called out their long quavering cry : " Tecolli, Teco-o-o-o-l-li ! " The sick man moved, opened his eyes, and looked about him, and as he did so the door swung back and Xicaltetecon entered.

" Alone ! " she cried, breathlessly, " and old Trinidad swore to me upon her rosary that she would not leave you a step ! Querido mio, pobrecito mio," and with the tears starting from her eyes, the girl seized the burning hand of the man who lay upon the bed. He looked vaguely at her at first, not understanding. Then a glad light shone for a moment in his eyes, and he drew her brown hand to his lips and kissed it softly, murmuring : " My little chicken, my little rabbit, my little mouse."

" Do not speak, Carlos," she whispered, bending over and putting her lips to his forehead. " Let me tell you this. To-night there will be medicine for you, medicine that will make you well and strong again, my Carlos. And I have paid a great price for it ; but you will forgive me, amado." She fell upon her knees by the bedside, still holding his hand, and hid her face in the covers. The sick man smiled faintly and stroked her dark hair.

The shadows were creeping into the room when she arose. She smoothed his pillow and arranged the disordered covers upon his bed. Then she went out into the little shed in the patio and fanned the ignited charcoal under the iron pot till it roared like the fire in a blacksmith's forge. It had grown dark when she reëntered the room with a smoking cup of broth in her hand. The sick man drank and fell back upon his pillow with a sigh, his eyes soon closing in the coma of the fever. Xicaltetecon did not light a taper, a bundle of which lay upon the table, but drew a chair to the bedside, and sat there, gazing into the darkness, with widely strained eyes.

Her body was broken by fatigue and her brain wearied to numbness by the agony of it all, stupefied by the inevitable, as that of a condemned man the night before execution. She listened to the breathing of the man who lay

beside her, growing more labored, more ster-
torous, as the hours of the night were marked
out of the present into the past by the bells of the
tower.   Perhaps she slept, but when the clock
struck ten she found herself mechanically counting the strokes, and the sound seemed to jar a
window in her brain, which flew open and she
saw the past,—how she had met him out there
by the mine, whither she had gone to sell fruit
and necuayotl to the men who labored and
dreamed therein.   *He* was standing by the
mouth of the shaft, clad in blue shirt and
trousers spotted with the yellow clay, and his
long hair glinted like gold in the sunlight under a
curious hat, such as no Mexican had ever worn.
He had looked at her and smiled and said:
"Adios, chiquita," with uncouth Northern ac-
cent, and she had laughed, drawing her rebozo
more closely about her face.   Thereafter they
had met one evening by the acequia, whither
she had gone for water, and he, the blond god,
had put his arm about her and kissed her, whis-

pering that she was more beautiful than the velvet-cloaked Madonna over the altar in the little church. Then to her the heavens had glowed as if with the fires of a mightier sun, and she had been glad with the gladness of angels. She had been as faithful to him as the dog to its master, wondering and worshipping, singing the day long of the coming night which would bring him home to her from the mine. He never went out with the men to the cantinas, but after nightfall he was wont to close the door tightly and pore over the letters and papers the stagecoach brought him, explaining to her, as she sat by his side, the great world he had left, and which she knew must be filled with noise and clamor and all distraction. Then he would draw her upon his knee, her arm would creep about his neck, their lips would meet,

" And overhead there shook a silver star."

. . . . The picture grew dimmer and she slept again.

"Xicaltetecon!" The word penetrated to her brain like a spear driven, and at the same time she felt a hand upon her arm. She opened her eyes and saw the figure of the rayed sun that hung between the breasts of Nantli Colotl glowing in the darkness. What was it? Why was the priestess there? But it all came back more quickly than the lightning of the rainless storms strikes upon the barren peak of Peñon Grande.

"Nelli, it is well," she said, springing to her feet. "Wait till I make light." She crossed the room, and, after fumbling in a drawer, struck a wax match and lit two of the yellow tapers. As the flame of the sputtering wicks grew brighter, she saw the priestess standing by the bed of the sick man, bending over to see his face.

"Ca, ca!" exclaimed Nantli Colotl; "it is time I came! A day more and all the power of Quetzalcoatl, the greatest of the gods, and the virtues of the sacred plant, could not have saved him from the shadows of Miquiliztli."

The priestess held in her hand a small jar, which she placed upon the table, and then threw aside the long zarape in which her tall form had been draped.

"Now, quick," she said, turning to the girl who stood waiting by her side ; "give me rags of cotton cloth the size of thy hand."

Xicaltetecon seized a white garment from a nail and tore it into bits. The priestess dipped a wooden spoon into her jar and spread the thick, viscid contents upon each piece of cloth, which she at once applied to the body of the sick man, continuing the operation until his entire body and face were completely covered with these plasters. She rolled him in the blankets and zarapes which were upon the bed, and threw everything else she could find in the nature of covering upon him. Some of the paste she forced into his mouth, and, taking one of the tapers, burned more of it under his nostrils, compelling him to inhale the pungent vapor.

"Quix ! Qualli !" ("It is done ! It is good !")

exclaimed the priestess ; and then, looking at the stars that glittered in the cold sky : "It is midnight. At three the medicine must be taken from him, or it would kill him. I will wait till then. Xitlapacho in tletl" ("Put out the light"), "Xicaltetecon."

The girl extinguished the tapers, and the priestess, drawing closely about her the long zarape, crouched down in a corner, leaning her head against the wall. Xicaltetecon threw herself upon a chair by the table, and buried her head in her arms. Not a sound broke the silence without. The round moon, climbing up the sky, cast its beams through the barred windows, and even to the bed whereon lay the fevered man, whose breathing was now inaudible.

The bells struck two. Xicaltetecon arose, and seeing that the priestess slept, crept over to the bed, and, bending down, kissed her lover's lips, well knowing that such kiss meant death to her. She whispered something to him (as if in his deep stupor he could hear), the last farewell to the living of the one about to die. She told him all that was in her heart, all the wondrous mysteries of a woman's boundless love ; the same in every clime, rare though it be. Then as the clock struck three she rose, awoke the priestess, and without a word opened the door and passed out into the night.

"Tell me again, Pedro, and if I find you have lied to me I will shoot you down like a dog ; and you know that the jefe politico is a friend of mine, and would not trouble me on account of your death."

The speaker was a man from the North, who spoke with little mercy of grammar the soft Southern tongue. He sat by the door of the adobe house, swathed in heavy zarapes, his pale face showing in strong contrast to the bright colors of the blanket.

The one whom he addressed was a typical Mexican of the lower class, clad in cotton shirt and trousers, his peaked felt hat on the back of his head.　His dark complexion and thick lips indicated his Otomé origin.

"I swear it is true, Don Carlos, by the soul of my mother and by the cross," replied the peon, earnestly.　"You may ask every one in the village and the padre himself.　It is as I told you. Two weeks ago to-day—'twas the day of San Antonio—she left your house and went to live with José, the arriero.　He boasted of it, Señor, at the cantina, and I myself saw her at the door of his hut, not once, but twice.　And a week ago she herself was stricken with the fever, the folgorante, Señor, that kills like the lightning, and the next day she was dead."

"Go on, Pedro."

"Bueno, Señor.　That night José and I carried her to the Campo Santo, and buried her outside the wall—for as you know, Don Carlos, she was not of the Church, and could not be put in holy ground—on the other side, near the clump of huisache trees."

"Yes?"

"And we wrapped her in the blue zarape, and" (here the peon lowered his voice) "I took one of your empty wine bottles, Señor, and filled it with holy water from the font in the church, and sprinkled it on her. You will not tell the padre, Don Carlos? For if he knew it he would curse me and make me bring him a load of wood from the Sierra for penance."

"Está bien, Pedro," said Don Carlos, rising slowly and painfully to his feet ; "I think I am strong enough to walk there with your help. So, let me rest on your arm."

Slowly the two men walked along the dusty street, in the slanting rays of the setting sun. At their doors the people gave Don Carlos kindly greeting: "Buenas tardes, Don Carlos ;" "Adios, caballero." It was not far to the little Campo Santo, where the orthodox natives of Tezcomaya continued their dreaming after death. Arrived at the iron gate which but made pretence of closing the holy ground to the outer world, for there was no fence about it, they did not enter, but turned to the right, and a few steps brought them to the cluster of low, graceful huisache trees which had sprung up, no one knew why or how, from the baked, waterless clay.

"Allá, Señor," said the peon, pointing to a low mound, at one end of which a piece of board, a rare and precious thing in this land, had been stuck into the ground. Nothing had been written upon it, for neither José, the arriero, nor Pedro knew how to write, and they dared not ask the padre.

"It is well, Pedro ; leave me here a while, and go you and wait for me at the gate of the Campo Santo."

"Si, Señor," and the peon turned obediently and walked away.

"Ah, little one," said Don Carlos, this time in his own tongue, for he was speaking to himself, "I had believed in you as I had never believed in woman. You were the only thing I ever loved, and yet when hope of my life was gone, you fled to another, not even waiting till the breath had left my body." He laughed, a laugh that was akin to a sob. "And yet why should I blame you? Why ask more of you, poor child, than of the women of my own land? Nay, sleep soft and sweet to all eternity, little Xicaltetecon."

The Water Lady

" And there are some that shimmer with the blue of heaven,
and these speak of love."

The
Water
Lady

O HÉ ! Hombre !"

The peon, at the call, dropped his shovel
and looked up. He saw a tall, blond-bearded
man bestriding a black horse, and behind him
another horseman mounted upon a handsome
gray, leading two pack mules. The dress and
arms of the one who spoke, as well as the embroidered saddle upon which he sat, told of
authority, so the peon took off his ragged straw
hat and answered : " Si, señor."

" Tell me, man, what place is that ? " spoke the
horseman, pointing to a straggling collection
of huts that speckled the sand about a mile
away.

"Jesus Maria, señor," answered the peon, twirling his straw hat.

"And where is Concepcion ?"

"Quien sabe, señor ?"

"Look here, my man !" said the horseman, with a slight impatience in his tone, though he knew how fruitless it was to be angry with these people ; "it means a *real* for you to know, and the devil's own time if you don't.   Sabes ?"

"You mean the city of Concepcion, señor ?" queried the peon, eying the silver piece which the other held in his fingers.

"Yes, if you want to call it a city."

"Bueno, señor.   It lies over there, but there's no trail, and if you want to be sure you had better go to the gulf and follow along the beach."

"And where lies the gulf?"

"Over there about two leagues, and then, by the scratched leg of your horse, two leagues more to Concepcion."

The horseman tossed the peon the silver piece

and turned his horse's head in the direction indicated by the native.

"I've got my bearings now," he said, speaking in English to himself. "We're below Concepcion, and not above it as I feared ; for it's Bonita's right foreleg that is scratched, which means to the right and north after we strike the shore."

He pricked his horse into a gallop, his long sword clinking against the silver buckles as the animal rose and fell, and his servant followed close behind, urging on the pack mules. They sped over the sandy plain, which swelled here and there into hillocks, held together by bunches of coarse grass, flecked with the livid green of the prickly pear. The blots of Jesus Maria were soon lost to view, and on every side the dreary waste was patched to the clouds. A half-hour's ride and a faint breeze blew cool upon the horseman's face. "Salt," he muttered ; "we have only to follow our noses now to reach blue water." He glanced back, and seeing that the pace was too hot for his mules, drew rein into a jog trot.

Now the low roar of the heaving, curling water came to his ear ; then he saw a narrow line of deeper blue than the sky, which broadened out as he neared it into the Gulf of California. The waters shimmered and danced in the sunlight, rolling heavily about the long sand-spits which stretched out into the cool waves like the parched tongues of the land. The rider dismounted, and, taking off his hat, drew deep breaths of the wind. The horse snorted at the sight of water, tugging at the bridle which its owner still held in his hand. The man laughed. "Try it if you want to, you landlubber," and he led the animal to the water's edge. It plunged its nose into a pool, but drew it quickly out, and turned its round soft eyes to its master with a look of amazement and reproach.

"José, we will let the animals rest for half an hour, and then follow along the beach to Concepcion."

"Si, Don Vicente." The servant dismounted, and, taking the bridle of his own horse and that of his master's, stood holding them, while the pack mules, fastened by a lariat to the saddle-peak, brought their noses together and stood patiently blinking at the vast sheet of scintillating blue.

Don Vicente threw himself down upon the shell-strewn sand, and, lighting a cigarette, blew clouds of smoke into the sky, watching the while the antics of white gulls that flew screaming above him.

The time up, they were again in the saddle, trotting along the beach, so close to the waves that at times the foam-fringed water shot up about the hoofs of the horses. Brown and long-legged snipe ran on ahead of the cavalcade, with plaintive "weep, weep," rarely taking wing; and small pink crabs sank into the sand, leaving a hole and a bubble.

It was a good hour's ride ere the low houses of Nuestra Señora de Concepcion (to give the ancient place its full name) rose into view, wedged in at the head of a narrow bay, up which the long surges, pushed by wind and tide, rolled foam-crowned and menacing. The white beach that spread out like a fan in front of the village was bestrewn with the long, flat-bottomed boats of the pearl-divers, hauled up beyond the reach of the waters. Beyond the town, on a sandhill, rose the cathedral, gray and pink in the sun-light, capped with bell-tower, while beyond and close to the gulf were the crumbling walls of an old monastery, long since abandoned by its holy tenants.

Entering the town and winding along a nar-row street, Don Vicente drew rein in front of a square, single-storied house, which a blue sign with white lettering proclaimed to be the Inn of the Three Pearls ; and this anyone who could not read might see for himself in the three blotches of white, shaded with pink and green and spawn-ing long rays of yellow paint.

The arrival of a stranger in this ancient and

musty town was something which had not occurred a score of times within the memory of man, and the bronzed natives gathered close in the narrow street, silently and respectfully admiring.

The owner of the hostelry, one Don Pablo Perez, a short stout man with saffron face and bristling mustache, affectionately known to his wife as El Perezoso (the lazy one), stood blinking at the door.

"My poor house is yours," he repeated, bowing mechanically, as the stranger swung himself from his horse ; and then, when the landlord saw the new-comer's face close to his own, he exploded : "By the glory of God ! It is Don Vicente himself ! *The* Don Vicente !" and his fat body was stricken as with galvanism. He bounded like a rubber ball to the horse's bridle. "Pedro ! Mateo ! You sons of Satan ! His Excellency's horse and baggage ! Manolita !" he yelled, turning houseward that his voice might carry through the open door, "'tis His

Excellency the Americano of the North. Be quick and stir thy big legs, Manolita."

A dozen natives sprang forward to hold the horse and assist in unloading the patient mules under the direction of Don Vicente's servant, while a thick-set woman of pure Andalusian blood appeared at the door, her dark eyes dancing with excitement.

"Hold thy noise, Pablo!" she exclaimed; "there is no need to destroy His Excellency's hearing with thy shrieking. This way, Excellency. You shall have the best room, the one you had last time, and I will send for my cousin's feather pillow for your head. Will you have a chicken or a kid killed?"

"A chicken will do for to-day, Señora," said the guest, smiling at the warmth of his reception, "but roasted, *asado*, you know, and in a clean pan without the taste of onions."

"Si, Si, Señor. Manolita forgets nothing; and if 'twere not for her, God only knows where the fonda would be by this time, with only such a lump of nothing as her husband to care for it."

"Perhaps in the *fondo* of the gulf," replied Don Vicente, laughing at his own pun, as the matron led the way to the low-ceiled room, which, with its furnishings, was the pride of the village.

"There, Don Vicente, you will sleep like an angelito here," she said, ushering him in. "See the new blanket I bought at La Plaz for sixteen reales, though, by the soul of my mother, I could get it in Michoacan for eight. The way they rob the poor here is an unhappiness to the saints in paradise."

She chattered on, while the traveller, seating himself upon the low bed, unscrewed his heavy silver spurs, hanging them on one of the wooden pegs that were driven into the wall. Then, after washing his face and hands in a pannikin of water, he lit a cigarette and strolled out into the patio, where Don Pablo sat impatiently awaiting him, in company with a bottle and two glasses.

"You must forgive my wife, Don Vicente; a green parrot is nothing to her for noise," said the host, rising. "No one has smelled of this tequila since you were here last year, and a cup of it is good for ten years of life."

"Salud, amigo," replied Don Vicente, emptying his glass of the transparent liquor at a single gulp. "What is there new?"

"Mucho, mucho, Don Vicente. I must talk with you long and seriously after your meal, for it concerns a compatriot of yours who came here four months ago,—perhaps a friend, quien sabe?"

"His name?" queried Don Vicente.

"God knows. I will go and get the book and you can read it for yourself. Here we called him Don Fernando."

"Tell me the story now," said the American, "for Doña Manolita has just caught her chicken, and it will be a long time before it is served."

The innkeeper drained his glass, and, accepting a cigarette proffered by Don Vicente, settled himself back in his straw-bottomed chair. "You must know, Señor," he began, after lighting his cigarette with a double-ended Mexican match and putting the unburnt piece back in his box for future use, "that this Don Fernando came here in May—yes, it was May. He was tall—not so tall as you, but with hair and eyes the same color as yours. He had a couple of burros carrying his baggage, and was seemingly possessed of much money in good Mexican silver pieces, together with some paper bills on Hermosillo which I did not like, but sent on to my brother in Sonora, and he said they were good as gold. We gave him your room, and Manolita fed him on chickens and kids and made him some real bread, for, like you, he hated tortillas. He stayed on and on, paying me three good silver dollars a week for his board. He amused himself going out with the pearl fishers, and would dive better than any of them. Old Tiburcio, the best diver of the lot, told me the Americano could stay under water longer than any native, though he scarce ever troubled to bring up an oyster, and the sharks never seemed to molest him."

Don Pablo poured himself out another glass of tequila, held it up to the light, and, then taking a sip, continued : "He was pale when he came, and coughed, but he grew better quickly ; and when he disappeared he was strong and hearty as myself, though not so fat.   Every day he was in the water, and the divers said he was searching for the great pearl which my father, Juan Perez, of blessed memory, once found and lost again, but I know better.   Bueno, one day he went off in his boat with old Pacheco, and when out by the island of Los Tiburones dived, and, Dios de mi alma ! never came up again !   Old Pacheco swore to it, and the men in the other boats that were near saw it, as well.   Po-brecito !"

Here Don Pablo helped himself to another glassful from the white bottle, and to another cigarette from the package which Don Vicente had left upon the table.

"So the poor fellow is dead!" said the American; "gone unshriven into the stomach of a shark, I suppose."

Don Pablo looked carefully about him and then drew his chair closer to that of his guest. "There are ears glued to the walls here, Señor, and we must speak low. Every one thinks him dead, but some curious things have happened. You know, Don Vicente, that I am like you, un hombre cientifico, materialista, positivista, and I do not believe in witchcraft, nor ghosts, nor the incantations of the divers to drive away the sharks. As for the priests, they are good enough for the women and children, but for men such as you and I, pah!" Don Pablo waved his hand in a gesture of infinite contempt. "Now, Señor," continued the narrator, "it was two days after his death, and I had made his clothing and books into a bundle, most carefully, and put them in that room, the one over there by the well, and one day this bundle vanished,—Si, Senor, vanished,—and in its place were six dollars, the sum

he owed me.   Now, no one came into the place
that day but an old woman, though my wife
says I was asleep and the devil himself might
have carried off the fonda.   The divers will all
swear that time and again since then they have
heard voices and laughter in the wooded isle of
Los Tiburones.   Old Panchita Guasta, who lives
in the ruins of the monastery and never owned a
tlaco, now comes and buys chickens, meat, and
fruit, paying for them with broad silver pesos.
'Tis a most difficult problem," continued Don
Pablo, scratching his head, ''and I can make
nothing of it.   But Don Fernando left some
papers, and a book full of writing in the English
language, I think, and these I have, for I had
locked them in the cupboard for safe keeping.
I will get them."

He bustled away and soon returned with a
package of papers and a small leather-bound
diary, all of which he gave to Don Vicente.   ''It
would be well for you to read these, Señor, and
find his residence and the name of his family, and

let them know of his death, for in spite of all, dead he must be. These divers are not to be believed in matters of ghosts, goblins, and miraculous virgins who ride upon the waves at night with pearls in their long hair, but in matters of fact they tell the truth ; and you know as well as I or any hombre cientifico that no man can live under the sea, and as for ghosts, 'tis folly, tonterias."

Here Manolita interrupted, carrying a smoking platter and a bottle of red wine. Don Pablo withdrew to bargain with a donkey driver for a load of onions.

His meal despatched, Don Vicente lit a cigar, and drawing up a chair put his feet upon it. Then he took up the diary, curious to learn what manner of man he might be, this countryman of his who had been devoured by the sharks, and who (what was much more curious) had been content to live in such a hole as Concepcion for so long a time. It was no easy matter to decipher the writing, for, owing doubtless to scarcity of paper in that benighted region, the writer had utilized an old diary after effacing the first script with bread or rubber. His pencil had marked but faintly at best, gliding now and then over a miniature pond of grease, without even a trace of its passage. The reader was interested, and managed to decipher here and there a word, but after a page or two the writing became clear and legible ; and thus it ran :

"May 6th.—I . . . peace . . . Concepcion . . . fresh eggs . . . fool . . . unutterable . . .

"May . . . the soughing of the waters lull . . . dreamless . . . but in me dull all creative . . . life here is but a vision seen in a trance . . . closer , . . nature . . . turmoil . . .

"May 9th.—Sometimes I dream, but it is all so misty and weblike that it will not bear the crystallization of a pen. The colors of the spectrum and more, from straight lines waving into

coruscant halos that dampen in turn into filmy
clouds when one would sense them into words.
These lines came to me to-day :

> And God breathed color, light, and sound,
>   And Silence spoke in music to the ear.
> In all the universe no man had found
>   Aught but himself to fear.

all of which is bad poetry, and I don't know
what I meant by it. I neither fear nor loathe
myself. I have lost *me ;* I have dissolved it into
nature like a lump of sugar in a jar of water.
There is nothing here, in the wide sky, the shimmering waters of the gulf, in these quaint primi-
tive folk, to make me bound back upon myself
and find my own personality. All this, however, is but the mooning of a convalescent.
Too weak to dominate our environment we float
with it, inmiscent.

"May 18th.—My strength leaps back in this
air, soft and humid, filled with the foam of the
salt sea. My muscles itch for action, but my

brain is quick wearied of work. To-day I took a plunge in the waves, in company with some white gulls that screamed discordantly at my splashing and nervously circled about my head. After the bath I felt like a Titan and ate like a Gorgon (did Gorgons eat ?).

"May 19th.—To-day is a feast day, devoted to the blessed memory of some saint who lived a thousand years ago, in Africa probably, about whom these fellows know nothing, and consistently celebrate him by doing nothing. That is, nothing but lay about the beach and yarn, I listening. There's matter for a dozen poems in their tales, but I cannot write now. Old Pacheco, bronzed, grizzled, perched on the side of a boat, tells the legend of the great pearl, alike the world over. Many have seen it at the sea bottom, glowing in the half-opened shell with light of its own. But just as one was about to seize it, it vanished—no, a small, delicate hand was stretched out and drew it quickly away, and the form of the Water Lady, Nuestra

Señora de las Aguas, could be seen fading into the depths, and before you could say "Jack Robinson" (supposing one could say anything under water) pearl, lady, and all had gone. Old Pacheco had seen her, and his father, likewise his grandfather—it seemed to run in the family. No mermaid, this Water Lady, no fish's tail, but a woman of fair form and feature. These folk had never heard of mermaids, otherwise they would have given her a tail, if only for the sake of historical consistency.

"May 20th.—The weekly stage-coach crawled in to-day, and the mail-sack was letterless for me, for which may the gods be praised. I hear nought, I want nought, of the outer world. This is liberty—pure, perfect. To-morrow I go pearl diving. I have hired old Pacheco and his boat for a month, and propose to walk about the bottom of the sea. To avoid unpleasant familiarity I have learned to use the double-pointed shark dagger. . . . To-day the white-maned horses of the gulf tide are too lively for safety . . . may to-morrow be calm, for I am all eagerness . . .

"May 22d.—Yesterday before sunrise we were off, paddling over a mirror-like sea with the sky in it. . . . Near the Isle of the Sharks (name of ill omen !), a foam-splashed acre of rock and earth covered with dense foliage, we cast anchor. Pacheco prepared the heavy iron weight and attached it to the rope. Naked, my shark dagger between my teeth, my feet upon the weight, and clutching the rope with my hands, I gave the word to the old man. . . . Down, down, with swiftness incredible, the water gurgling and humming in my ears, till I reached the bottom, twenty feet below the surface. I opened my eyes now and looked about me . . . the sunlight filtered through the water in waves of white and green light which trembled with the currents, revealing and shadowing in turn. A floor of hard white sand inlaid with shells of varied hue ; the brown and yellow glandina, open-mouthed, purpling within ; the flat and fanlike pectens ; the spiked murex, reddening into ruby as if with the blood of impaled fishes. Here and there gleamed a jewelled cypræa, like unto a lost bit of a queen's diadem. On every side rose huge sea plants with arms yearning to the light and air. The long leaves of the green algæ curled in the swirling tide like snakes, while the dreaded Campo Santo plant, so called because many a diver has been held in its hideous embrace, shot out its long red ribbons like amorous tongues eager to seize whatever might come within their reach. . . . Beyond were dark and mystic paths, losing themselves in shadows, leading to other realms of the deep, through which scaly and glistening forms, grotesque and uncouth, floated lazily or darted arrow-like in flight or pursuit. . . . It was strangely intoxicating, that life of the sea, the realm of mystery forbidden to man . . . strange and weird in the soft, solemn light, the infinite silence, and the clinging, pressing, lifting water. . . . It seemed an age that I stood there peering, till the almost bursting lungs gave warning, and I shot up into the air and sunlight, and was dragged half fainting into the boat by old Pacheco.

" By the mother of God, Don Fernando ! " he exclaimed, piously, " I had given up hope.   No diver on the coast ever remained longer below ! It was rash of you to try it, carramba ! "   My eyes stung for a long time, but the faintness passed quickly away, and, after clothing myself, I could do my share at the paddle as we sped homeward. . . .   In my sleep that night there passed before me visions of sea nymphs, bacchantes, and what not, circling in merry dance, half mocking, half pleading, as though I were some Gautama or Faustus to be led astray, though in good sooth 'twere no hard task for them.   Some bits of rhyme jingled through my head, the burden being

> Sing the sirens songs of no meaning
> As rocked on the waters they float,
> Guarding the pearl?

. . . but the rest is metrical din. I can imagine a number of things the sirens might sing if they chose to, but nothing very novel. . . . Mayhap 'twas a great poem, quien sabe? . . . To-day at noon I go out with Pacheco, and will dive again into the depths. They're as fascinating as the Venusberg.

"May 28th.—To-day I went down seven times, and the divers are amazed at the length of time I can stay under water. My watch, left in the boat with Pacheco, showed five minutes, something unheard of among them. I tore off and brought up some pearl oysters, to please the old Indian, who thought I must have good luck, buena suerte, but they contained but seed pearls, and these of poor quality and scarce any orient. While I was below, a huge shark swam close to me, staring at me with his small, devilish eyes. I held my dagger ready to plunge it into his cavernous mouth, but he had decided not to attack, and with a whisk of his tail vanished behind a clump of the Campo Santo plant.

.   .   .   Since I have used the oil on my body
and face before diving, my eyes do not pain me
any more.   .   .   .

"June 6th.—The days flash by, full of nothing;
empty, at least, of things distasteful.   Eden must
have been something like this—an endless sum-
mer time, full of things humming and buzzing
and droning, and little waves lapping and splashing, ticking time smoothly away.   .   .   .   I am
not even lonely, and yet   .   .   .

"June 12th.—I wonder if the gods make mad
those who enter a forbidden realm?   Was it fact
or phantasy   .   .   .   a day dream, a sugges-
tion?   .   .   .   If I write it out before me, I
may understand it better.   .   .   .

"This, then, is what I saw, or thought I saw
to-day, in the green depths, wherein I now
tread and float at will—a woman's face, weirdly
beautiful in the pale emerald light that shimmered from above, looked out at me from a
cluster of giant algæ.   One must think quickly
when one cannot breathe, and I leapt toward

her. As I did so she fled, and I caught a glimpse
of an exquisite form ere it disappeared into one
of the dark paths that led toward the rock
foundation of the Isle of the Sharks, for I was
then quite near it. I could not stay to follow,
but when I had mounted to the surface and
breathed, I plunged again, and sought her madly,
pushing on through the swaying algæ till I
reached the wall of rock, but in vain. Only a
swarm of foul bladder fish—owls of the sea—
flashed about me in blind struggle to escape.
. . . I cannot make it out. Is the legend of Our
Lady of the Waters true, as told by old Pacheco,
or was this form but a creation of my brain, projected upon the crystal background of the swirling waters? I could not see that face clearly,
yet every feature is clearly stamped upon my
memory. Were I a painter, I could now lay it
sharply with pigment upon canvas—the arching
brows; the deep, dark eyes; the full lips, lifted
at the corners into a smile; the long black hair
that spread out behind her as she fled; the swell-

ing hips and tapering limbs ; all these details are too concise for something that was but the wraith of a memory-conjured vision. . . . If I do not see her again I shall think I am going mad. . . . If I do not see her again I shall certainly go mad. . . . How sweet that sounds, ' Nuestra Señora de las Aguas ' . . . Ave, Ave, Maria !

"June 17th.—Five days of vain search, . . . an eternity ! . . . I am in doubt, nervous, irritable, possibly dyspeptic. I am wearying of Don Pablo and Doña Manolita and their incessant chatter, and of the inn of the Three Pearls, and cannot for the life of me understand what Concepcion was conceived for. . . . I shall drink a bottle of Don Pablo's wine before going to bed (it is good wine ; I wonder where the old rascal stole it ?).

"June 20th.—No, I am not mad, nor dreaming, nor calling spirits from the vasty deep which do not come when I do call. She is as real as anything in life, this lady of the waters ! . . .

I saw it, her, yes, *her*, again to-day, moving amidst the long, tremulous algæ. She saw me and waved her hands, calling. Again I sprang forward, again she vanished, melting into the deep shadows.

"June 22d.—I must leave this place, if I have a care for my own good. The divers themselves are beginning to have grave doubts as to my sanity. Why any one should wish to dive day after day, and not bring up a single oyster, is beyond the understanding of these folk. I see old Pacheco in deep converse with the rest, marking his talk with shrugs and sharp gestures. Perhaps they think I am searching for the great pearl. They are not far wrong. . . . But this thing, be it woman or devil, shall mock me no longer. . . . To-morrow I will sail across the gulf, in Pepe's fishing boat. . . . Perhaps afterwards I can make something of this that will be worth reading. . . . We write with our own blood . . .

"June 23d.—It is too hot to travel to-day, and

there is no wind to blow us across the gulf. So I sit in the patio and watch Doña Manolita rolling about, and listen to snatches of her gossip, wherein the Holy Virgin is much mixed with the price of onions and the depravity of chickens. The big square of sunlight moved over the patio and I recked naught of it, until at three the bell in the cathedral roared more loudly than usual.

"'Dios de mi alma!' exclaimed the stout hostess. ''Tis three already, and I not dressed!'

"'What is it, Madrecita?' I inquired lazily.

"'Ah, Señor, 'tis a special mass for the lay Sisters of Saint Joseph and they do penance,' and with this she disappeared. It is always cool in the shadowy aisles, beneath the great stone arches, and the smell of incense that hangs about the place is not rank to me. I believe I will climb the hill and see these sisters of St. Joseph, though I know they are not fair and they reek of garlic.

"Midnight.—I must write it down ere I sleep upon it, if sleep I may, for rather than rest I would bound out there in the moonlight, and thence into the cool waters, and swim about and splash, telling my joy to the night birds and scaly fish, shrieking my love to the moon. But write this I must, quietly, coherently. So, then, I went up to the cathedral, along the stone-paved calzada, verily a *via crucis* to tender feet. From under the arched door came the music of the mass, heavily, but thinning out in the open air. Cool within and dark by contrast, the thick shadows flecked with the flames of candles, the air heavy with incense that one smelled and tasted. The gold and tinsel upon the altar glittered, and the white-robed priest genuflexed, turned, bowed ; the bell tinkled ; the boys swung the censers ; above all gleamed the cross, *stella maris vitæ.*

"The sisters of Saint Joseph were kneeling upon the stone pavement, clad in long black robes that fell to their feet, with cowls that covered head and face. On their backs, suspended by broad red ribbon passing over either

shoulder, were illuminated pictures of Saint
Joseph himself, duly blessed. All these maids
and matrons moved about upon their knees,
crossed, bowed and murmured, rosary in hand.

" 'Dominus vobiscum. Ite, missa est.'

" The priest turned toward them and made the
sign of the cross; the music of the little organ
crept away under the arches. Then, whispering Aves and counting their beads, the black-
robed sisters began moving around the church,
still upon their knees, stopping before each small
altar and painted saint. The air was sibilant
with muttered invocations and heavy with the
smoke of liquidamber. In the shadowy recesses huddled the men of the village, some
pious of face and demeanor, others grinning de-
risively. I stood there, fascinated by the lights,
dreaming of formless things, I know not how
long. The sun, falling, shot level rays of light,
bands of golden dust, through the western windows, when, as with one accord, the women
stopped, arose, and made their way toward the

great doors that led outward. The younger men sprang forward to the font, and as each maid passed, well known, perhaps, in spite of cowl, gave holy water with their finger-tips. Now and then a cowl was raised enough to show black sparkling eyes, to tell something in a look; fingers were pressed for a rendezvous. Slowly the church emptied until I stood alone,—nay, not yet, for an old crone, cloaked and hooded as the others, bent double with age, and leaning upon a heavy staff, came tottering toward me. An impulse, perhaps of courtesy or pity, I know not what, moved me to dip my fingers into the font and hold them out toward her. From beneath the black folds she reached out a hand, wee and wondrous white, and touched my fingers. Then her bent figure straightened, the staff dropped clanging upon the stone floor. With a rapid movement she threw back the cowl, and before me stood the Water Lady, Nuestra Señora de las Aguas ! Ave, Ave, Maria !

6

"I felt akin to those torrents which, following a cloudburst, roll down the sandy bed of an arroyo, carrying all before them. I could have seized her then and there and borne her off to a keep, as did the barons of old when passion lived and sang and roared throughout the land, ere came the tinkling troubadour to tie the giant in silken rhymes. Mine! Not in the green depths of the sea, midst swaying algæ and tremulous weeds, where breath of life is not and dimmed sight deceives, but in the glad sunlight, on firm earth, under the arching blue. I put out my hands, and, as she drew back with a light laugh, I seized her cloak. 'No, no!' she timorously pleaded; 'to-morrow, in the sea, by the Isle of the Sharks, at noontide. Come to me then.'

"Was this some woman's trick to elude me? I grasped her cloak more firmly.

"'You shall not escape me again,' I cried in desperation.

"Fool that I was! With a movement more

rapid than thought she threw off her cloak, leaving it in my hands, and sped away like a frightened deer. I cast aside the garment with an oath and followed her as quickly as I could, clambering and stumbling over ancient chairs which I could scarce see in the shadows; but she reached the other end of the church ere I could seize her, and vanished within a small door that closed behind her. Before it barred her from my sight she gave me a look, one of mingled promise and reproach. I struck the door with all my strength, but the heavy wood yielded not a tremor to my blow. I would have called her, but I knew no name, only, 'Our Lady of the Waters.'

"I was still at the door, fumbling vainly for some key or bolt that might open it to me, when I felt a hand upon my shoulder. Turning quickly, I saw standing behind me the old priest. 'Why this violence in the house of God, my son?' he said sternly, but not unkindly.

"'A person passed that way, father,' I answered, not a little embarrassed, 'and I would have followed.'

"'And hadst thou then the right to follow?' There was a look of quiet amusement in the old man's eyes that told me he knew, or perchance guessed, the object of my pursuit.

"'I know not, father,' I answered. 'What is right?'

"'Ask that question of one wiser than I am,' said the priest, his face clouding in doubt, and folding his hands beneath his robe he turned away and walked slowly back to the sacristy.

"I ran out of the church by the great doors in front and looked down the stony calzada which led to the town, thinking perchance I might catch a glimpse of the blue-robed figure in the golden haze of the setting sun. But no! nothing; only old Pepe Huarto, the pearl diver, climbing wearily up, chewing a piece of 'sparto grass.

"'Pepe,' I exclaimed, 'hast thou seen any one come out of the church?'

" 'When, Señor?' he inquired, staring stupidly at me.

" 'Just now, a moment ago, a woman.'

" 'Si, Don Fernando, a woman came out of the sacristy door on the left there, and fled as if the devil were after her—or the priest,' he added, with a sly look.

" 'And which way did she go?' I inquired eagerly.

" 'That way,' he said slowly, pointing with his finger to the ruins of the old monastery more than two miles away, 'to where she lives, Señor.'

" 'You know her, then, Pepe mio?'

" 'I did not look with great care, Señor, for 'twas no business of mine, but I think, I am sure, it was the little Dolores, the daughter of the old witch who lives in the ruins.'

" I looked again in the direction of the monastery and caught sight for an instant only of a blue speck on the top of a sand hill. I could not overtake her then, for surely she was swifter of foot than I, and I must rest upon her promise; so I seized Pepe by the arm, and with my other hand drew a Mexican cigar, which I thrust into his eager paws. 'Come and sit by me here, Pepe,' and I led him to a stone seat near the church, from whence I could see the ruins, black against the setting sun, 'and tell me all you know about Dolores. To-morrow you shall drink the best bottle of wine that El Perezoso has in the fonda.'

" ' Well, then, Don Fernando,' said the old man, lighting the cigar and drawing two or three long whiffs of smoke into his lungs, 'there is not much to tell. It is this way. Pedro Guasta, whom I knew as well as any one knew him, and that is not much, was a diver like the rest of us. He was not born here, but came somewhere from the East, perhaps from Sonora or Chihuahua, quien sabe? He could read books and could talk better than the padre, when he talked at all, which was seldom. When he came here he brought with him his

wife and the chiquita. He took up his residence
in the old ruins, and it was said he knew strange
things about the old monastery, the way to un-
derground dungeons, and had found treasures
there, though, for a truth, he never showed signs
of having either silver or gold. He was poor as
the rest of us, eating only to his fill when he
brought in a pearl to the father of Don Pablo
Perez, who was a robber of the poor, Señor, and
paid the men but a tenth of the value of their
finds, till the saints in paradise grew weary of it
and let the devil take him one night to hell.
This father of Don Pablo——'

"'Never mind him, Pepe,' I interrupted, 'go
on with Guasta.'

"'Bueno, bueno, Señor. Well, a few years
ago Guasta died of the fever, or of something else,
and was not buried in holy ground. He left his
widow and the chiquita Dolores to get along as
best they could, and the saints only know how
they do it, though now and then the old witch
brings in a pearl and trades it with Don Pablo,

who is more of a thief than his father. It is a rare thing that one sees Dolores about the town. She is more beautiful than the Virgin over the altar, but the young men about here are afraid of her, I know not why.'

"Here Pepe stopped and seemed to be considering if there were anything more of interest he could tell. 'They say, Don Fernando,' he added, after a moment's pause, 'that the old monks built a passage way under the sea from the monastery to the Isle of Los Tiburones,' and he pointed to the green blot that lay upon the water below us, like an emerald set in turquoise.

"'It is a thing the ancestors tell (cosas de abuelos), and I do not tell you that it is true, Don Fernando.'

"I strained my eyes again in the direction of the monastery and thought I saw the blue speck again crossing the space of white sand that lay before the gray walls. Old Pepe, seeing that I cared to ask him nothing more, arose, and doffing his hat, said: 'Hasta mañana, Señor.'

" 'Hasta mañana, Pepe,' I answered, 'and do not forget the bottle of wine at the fonda.' . . .

" *Hasta mañana!* How will I live till to-morrow? Dolores! thy sweet face will haunt my dreams, should I sleep this night. What manner of strange child art thou, Dolores, who hast been cast among these poor folk? I will meet her to-morrow, in the green waters, amidst the swaying algæ and the tremulous reeds. . . .

"June 25th. There are chapters in men's lives that are closed and sealed with a seal, that they may not be read by mortals. Some of these are written by pens of iron dipped in blood, others by quills of gold inked in the blue of the sky, and the reading thereof aloud is like the murmur of waters passing over round pebbles. The music of her voice is still in my ears and the touch of her kisses is yet upon my lips. In these moments time and space were not, and the pain-mingled sands of life stopped running through the glass of eternity. (Has it ever been so with you, O brother?) . . .

" It was near noon when I rowed out to the Isle of the Sharks, a light breeze ruffling the water into glinting lines. What ails thee, Pacheco? Bend to thy paddle, man. Are the hinges of thy arms and knees growing rusty with age? . . . I needed not the old man's help to adjust the weights to my feet. . . . We had cast anchor by the Isle of the Sharks, a score of yards from the shore, at the place where I had first met her. . . . In a moment I was ready and had been lowered into the cool water and sped down into its opalescent depths. Once upon the hard white sand I looked about me, peering eagerly into the shadows, making my way carefully but rapidly along one of the paths that seemed to lead toward the rocky barrier that supported the green isle. I soon saw her coming, gliding toward me, cleaving the water like a fish. She took my outstretched hand in hers. At that instant, although it seemed to me I had scarce been half my usual time beneath the sea, my lips and lungs gave way and bubbles passed before my eyes. My sight grew dim, there was a strange drumming in my ears, I was moving rapidly through the water . . . there was a sense of suffocation, blinding lightning flashed before my eyes. Then a blank. . . . God! what pain! My chest seemed to be rent asunder, and pangs beyond human endurance shot through every limb as if I had been stretched upon the rack. . . . This is what they call the agony of death, thought I, the spirit tearing itself from the body . . . now it is over. . . . I am resting quietly, peacefully, but I am so tired. . . . What a delicate tracery! Some artist of wondrous skill has painted flowers and the leaves of trees on glass, through which one sees the blue sky and an exquisite imitation of fleecy clouds . . . and the clouds are moving . . . something is put to my lips and I feel that I am drinking. How curious that one should drink when one is dead, and yet it seems as if I had a body and new life were thrilling through it. . . . Now the sky and the clouds, the leaves and the flowers, fade away, and I am sleeping . . . am I dreaming? . . . I know that face, but cannot think where I have seen it before . . . it is a beautiful face, coming between me and the sky, a woman's face, with soft, sweet, tender eyes that are looking into mine. . . . Why can I not remember . . . it seems important that I should. . . . Those are wonderful eyes! I can trace the perfect arch of the dark brow upon the white skin ; long black hair hangs down and brushes against my face ; the red lips, half parted, showing two rows of even white teeth . . . if I could only move now I could touch those lips, but I am too lazy to think it all out and I don't know how to move . . . bits of sunlight seem to strike down through the tracery of leaves and flowers upon her white body . . . sunshine? . . . clap, lap, lap, is that sound? . . . water? . . . the sea ! . . . old Pacheco? . . . the boat !

. . . the wheel of memory begins to turn again . . . *Dolores!*

"My lips move at this word, I speak it aloud; and the sweet eyes smile, the red lips come down to me and press my own. The tide of life flows back, bounding.

. . . . . .

"The sun is slanting over the waters. In the boat sits old Pacheco, a bit of rope in his hand, gazing about him and waiting, the tears streaming down his tanned and weather-beaten cheeks. He's muttering something to himself . . . prayers for the soul of Don Fernando? Hours have passed and he is still waiting for his master to come up from the deep sea; for his master, who is upon the Isle of the Sharks, looking at him through the thick foliage. . . . We peer at him together, laughing pityingly, but softly, for the stillness of eventide is upon the water and the slightest sound could be heard afar off. We stand upon that bank up which Dolores, with almost superhuman strength, had dragged me, fainting, drowning, but a few hours before. . . . A last embrace . . . only until to-morrow, *hasta mañana* . . . and I drop quietly into the water and swim under the leafy branches that bend over till they touch the waves, and then out to the boat. Pacheco does not see me until I am almost upon him. He hears me, turns, falls to trembling, and crosses himself; gives a cry of mingled fear, astonishment, and delight; then manages, not without difficulty, to drag me into the boat. I cut short his prayers and explanations.

" ' Pacheco,' I exclaim, ' you will swear to me by the memory of your mother and the most holy Virgin that you will say nothing of this, and I will give you fifty pesos in silver to buy a dozen donkeys for your son to carry goods up into Sonora.'

"He swore it, and I think the old man will keep his word. Dolores ! "

The remaining pages of the diary were quite

illegible. Either the pencil of the writer had needed sharpening or the paper had refused to be marked by its point.

Don Vicente closed the little book, and while he was pondering that which he had read, Don Pablo approached softly. He noted that his esteemed friend was solemn, even triste, muy triste, and knowing but one panacea for sorrow, he waddled off and returned in a moment with a fresh bottle of tequila and two glasses, all of which he compassionately, reverently, placed in front of his honored guest.

Mechanically the hand of Don Vicente took the bottle and poured a glassful of the transparent liquor. He was old and worldly-wise, was Don Vicente, and he sighed as he lifted the glass to his lips, "Pretty, very pretty, but how long will it last?"

The Mysterious Disappearance of Mrs. T. Tompkins Smith

The Mysterious Disappearance of Mrs. T. Tompkins Smith

THE train pulled out of the frontier station with a clanging of iron, midst a clamor of voices, both sounds blending and vanishing, as it gathered headway, into the smooth hum of the speeding wheels. The sun, scarce risen above the horizon, marked black blotches of shadow upon the white arid plain just under the writhing cactus and stunted palms, though there was yet in the air something of the cool breezes of the night.

Straight as twin arrows cast from a single bow, the two lines of shining steel converged till they met the sky, far to the south, then sped on till they reached the White City, fetters of conquest upon the desert. Puffs of wind whirled the dust into inverted pyramids, and sent them spinning away in fantastic dance.

The conductor entered the third-class car, where he began lustily calling for "boletos!" The half-sleeping, blanketed Mexicans, lazily bestirred themselves to drag out the bits of paper entitling them to ride on the iron way. Thence he passed into the Pullman, assuming an expression of easy and familiar joviality. It was "tickets, please," here—the English language and politeness corresponding to first class.

"Ah! Mrs. Tibbins, glad to see you back again," he said, as he registered a pass tendered by an overdressed and somewhat vulgar woman of the common American type. "Been havin' a good time in the States?"

The woman smirked.

"Well, I should say!" she remarked, putting her pass back into a red wallet. "I tell you, Mr. Crosby, it does a power of good to one to get a breath of fresh livin' air after bein' down to Mexico for four years. Gracious ! I have had enough of this place, I have."

"Might be worse though," sighed Mr. Crosby, half resenting the remark and half sympathizing with the sentiment, for he had lived in Mexico for many years. He turned to the other side, taking long strips of red tourist tickets from two elderly persons, buried amid a heap of baskets and satchels, and whose dress proclaimed the female sex.

"I am Mrs. Myra Tilden," croaked one of them, "that's my name written on the ticket. I'm from Mauchunk, going to do Mexico."

"Certainly, ma'am," replied the conductor, clipping the tickets with his punch.

"Conductor, when do we get to the dinner station ?" groaned the other fossil as the man turned away.

"One forty-five."

"Thanks."

The train was now gliding rapidly over the

white desert of caliche.   The sky, unflecked by a single cloud, burned to a gray that seemed to shimmer in waves of heat.

As the conductor approached, a young man aroused himself sufficiently from the perusal of a yellow-covered novel to extend his ticket, though without taking his eyes from the book.

Only three more passengers, sitting together at the end of the car.   As the conductor neared them he became more deferential, for there was a flavor of the stockholder about the men, and a chic about the dark blue costume of the woman, that bespoke the upper circles.

"Going through?" queried Mr. Crosby, pleasantly.

"Yes.   We are due in the city day after to-morrow night, are we not?" asked one of the gentlemen, handing two tickets, while the other produced a pass.

"Afternoon, sir, at two o'clock."

The lady looked up.

"Two days more of this!" she exclaimed,

with some impatience in her tone. " Really, Tom, the play is not worth the candle."

"My dear," replied the person addressed, "you would come, you know, though Mr. Jarr told you it was a horrible trip. Long, dusty, bad eating, and all that, you know."

" Yes," she assented, wearily, "that's all very true." She opened her valise, and, taking therefrom a book, leaned back against the pillow which the fee-expecting negro porter had placed behind her.

" You'll excuse us, my dear, if we go to the smoking-room for a cigar?"

She nodded acquiescence, without looking up, and the two men walked away.

Soon the book fell, and Mrs. T. Tompkins Smith leaned her elbow on the window-sill and her chin on her hand, gazing out at the flying desert and the distant gnarled hills that rose abrupt, as if man-built. The dull white was a background for her thoughts ; there were clouds of dun dust too, whereon she could image at her will.

But they broke in upon her reverie. The ancient female tourists had been deeply impressed by the statement of the young woman to the effect that she had lived long in Mexico, and ventured questioningly :

" Tough ? Well, I guess. Why, there ain't a decent house, nor a stove, nor a chimney in the whole city. Cook ? Oh, yes, with charcoal on stones with holes in them. Oh, 'tain't so hard ; you get used to it after a while. Society ? Well, of course I have to go into it, as I live there. It ain't what we have at home. The Mexicans ain't much on society. Catholics ? Oh, yes, you *just ought* to see the churches ! "

She rattled on, sharp in voice, a tone that cut like the shrieking of a file.

Mrs. T. Tompkins Smith would have given gold to stop her ; turned to freeze her into silence with a glance, encountering only her back, on which the icy shaft broke harmless.

The lady resumed her position at the window, shutting out the voice by an effort of the will, drowning it in the whirring of the wheels. She thought of nothing, in the stupor of widely strained eyes, in the gentle rocking of steel springs.

Suddenly she became aware of a mirage, surely one of those phantasms she had read about, occurring in deserts. A gigantic horse, higher than the distant hills, bore toward her with ponderous gallop a gigantic rider whose head scraped the skies. She noted every detail of the horseman's costume, though the face was indistinct. He wore leggings of brown leather, tight fitting, trimmed with silver buttons adown the sides ; a jacket of blue, faced with silver ; and a peaked hat of gray, about which curled a golden cord. She could see the embroidered saddle-cloth, the shining butts of the pistols that stuck out of the holsters, the long machete that swung by his side. The rider was waving a white handkerchief, like a scudding cloud, frantically hailing.

Nearer came the monstrous forms, until the

forefeet of the horse were upon the very car, and, oh !—Mrs. T. Tompkins Smith gave a little start and the mirage vanished, but left a comparatively small and very solid kernel of reality, for she could now see a horse and rider of natural size, and scarce a mile from the train, galloping madly toward a point somewhat beyond it, as if to head it off.

Surely a man in the desert was like a castaway at sea, flying likewise a signal of distress. Mrs. T. Tompkins Smith acted upon the impulse. "Conductor !"

"Yes, ma'am." The worthy put down a novel belonging to one of the passengers and came toward her.

"There is a man on horseback over there trying to stop the train." She indicated with her jewelled finger.

Mr. Crosby looked, studied for a moment, then seized the bell-rope, pulling it steadily thrice, bringing the train to a standstill.

"I'm sure that's Don Federico himself !" he

exclaimed excitedly.   "Lucky I saw him in time !"

"Who is he, Mr. Crosby?" eagerly queried the file, gathering with the ancient tourists at the car window.

"Well, he's a big man, I can tell you," vouchsafed the conductor.   "Lives about six hundred miles down the road here. Has a silver mine that pays him millions a year, and a regular castle near the Nevada de Toluca volcano— helped build this road and owns part of it." This hastily, and he then rushed out of the car to explain the signal to the engineer and receive Don Federico.

The horseman reined in his panting animal at the very steps of the car and, swinging himself from the saddle, proceeded to unbuckle the girths, answering at the same time the salutations of the conductor and porter, who had gathered officiously about him.

"Put this saddle in the express car, this valise in my berth. Get a bucket of water for the horse." They flew to execute his orders. The animal having drained the last drop of the precious fluid, its owner gave it a sharp cut with his short riding-whip and the order "Á casa !" and the horse, now riderless, sped away over the desert.

"Glad to see you, Don Federico. Take number six. It's the best section in the car. Anything else we can do for you, sir?"

He waved them away, taking off his heavy Mexican hat and hanging it upon one of the brass hooks. Then he turned to look about him.

Now a most singular thing occurred. The eyes of tall Don Federico fell upon Mrs. T. Tompkins Smith, who just at that moment was looking hard upon him, and for a time the two stood as if transfixed, gazing at each other, moving not outwardly, but the two hearts pumping blood at redoubled speed.

The file, seeing it all, tittered, and broke the spell. With long, quick stride Don Federico walked down the aisle toward Mrs. T. Tompkins Smith, his hand extended.

"Margaret ! Surely it is you !" Then hesitatingly, remembering, "I beg pardon—Mrs.—eh—Mrs.——"

"T. Tompkins Smith." This loudly and sonorously, as if revelling in Tompkins and glorying in Smith ; then she added, cordially putting her hand in his : "I knew you almost at once, Fred, in spite of your costume and tan. Have you really become a Mexican, and are you really the great Don Federico?" She spoke quickly, to smother embarrassment. Her voice trembled, for the past fell upon her like an avalanche. In her parlor, at home, flanked by a tea-table and bric-a-brac, buoyed up in a perfect gown, she would have known just the proper things to do and say ; but here in the desert, on whirring wheels, it took time to adjust the present to the past.

Don Federico gazed in admiration at the woman he had lost. The same form and face, splendid in their strength and beauty, the lines of the face a little firmer, more saddened perhaps. The calm eyes, deep and blue as a mountain lake, with volcanic possibilities, the wealth of brown hair knotted behind in careless fashion. Yes, she had changed but little, though it was a long sweep of time, full of action for him, and he felt as if the ages had piled up against him.

She waved him to the seat in front of her : "Tell me about it, will you ?"

He took no note of the tone, only heeding the words. The emotion of pleased surprise had faded, leaving bitter memories in bold relief, and his voice, as he replied, was two-edged with irony. "I will not say that I do not think it would interest you to know of my past : how plain Fred Hawthorne became Don Federico, in what to your eyes is rare and strange apparel ; and there is something romantic in picking a man up in the desert." He looked out of the window and then back at her face, which was hardening. "I suppose," he continued pensively, "it would all make a very interesting story, to be retailed as one of your Mexican experiences to a circle of admiring friends after your return. But really, you know, there is hardly any legitimate basis for a display of interest in my affairs on your part."

It was a slap in the face. She reddened, then paled. It pleased him to know that he had cut deeply. The lady looked about her to see if she could be overheard. The file and the fossils, awearied of staring at the new-comer and his companion, had assembled at the other end of the car and, heads together, were deep in words. Mr. T. Tompkins Smith and his companion, Mr. Jarr, were in the smoking compartment, comparing views on the subject of silver and exchange. Then she turned again to Don Federico, and burst forth like a torrent:

"There is an Italian proverb, Mr. Hawthorne, which says that the undeserved thrust glides harmless from the shield. Somehow, out here, the forced and the artificial jar on one. Can't we be truthful in the desert ? It seems to me I can. According to all precedent I should hate you, I suppose, and show my scorn for you in some tragic manner, and all that ; but I can't, Fred. Now I have put away the shield, strike again."

The man's mouth and eyes, curved in sarcasm, now lifted in wonderment.

"Hate me, Margaret ; you hate me ! What a strange twisting of things ! I, who worshipped you as I am sure no man ever worshipped a woman ! Hate me because you dismissed me like a cur from your doorstep ? Ah ! this is a strange world."

He smiled bitterly. He, too, had thrown away the shield, and they stood defenceless, face to face.

She bent over, seeking his eyes, a little pained smile upon her lips.

"Oh, Fred ! I thought we were to be truthful ! We have but a few minutes to talk here, after seven years of silence. Could anyone injure a woman more than you did me ?"

His wonderment grew.

"Do you mean to say, Margaret, that you never wrote the letter which struck me down like a felled ox, breaking our engagement, requesting me never to see you again, and announcing that you were to marry T.—eh— T.—T.——

"T. Tompkins Smith. Oh! yes. I wrote the letter, Fred; there is nothing so melodramatic in all this as a forged letter. I could not have done otherwise, very well, as you should admit, though," she added thoughtfully, "I might have left out the reference to T.—T.— T.——"

"Tompkins Smith!"

He, too, bent over, and his words came like rifle-shots.

"In God's name, then, how dare you look me in the face? I was poor, he rich! But you knew of my poverty long before that, and rich men were buzzing about you like bees around a pot of honey. Such action would not have sur-

8

prised me on the part of the average woman;
but you, Margaret—I had idealized you so much
above the rest ! You were to me the goddess
whose skirts would have been soiled at the touch
of others of your sex——"

It was the woman's turn for wonderment,
though her eyes flashed with indignation. "Do
you really mean to say, Fred Hawthorne, that
you do not know my reason for that letter ? Do
you believe it was on account of your poverty or
his wealth——" Her wrath strangled speech.

"I give you my word, Margaret, that I know
of nothing, absolutely nothing, that could have
given you cause to reproach me. I thought for
a moment some slander had been told you, but
you were not the woman to believe the tales of
others. I knew you too well, or thought I did,
to even consider that possibility."

She leaned back with a gesture of weariness.

"I never believed any tales of others. I
thought you knew, must have known, that I
saw you." She stopped, as if to see over again

that which she was about to tell. "It was the last time we met, the night of the Van Steen ball. You remember it, Fred? You had left me only an hour before I arrived there, and there was no prouder, happier woman than I in all that crush. I had put on my best frock and all my jewels, and was eager for men to say : 'See how beautiful she is ; she belongs to *him*.' You were there, Fred, head and shoulders above other men, and I was glad I looked well for your sake. Hardly an hour of that intoxication for me, for it was not eleven o'clock when I saw you in that little alcove with Mrs. Stanhope —*saw* it all, Fred. No, don't interrupt me." She held up her hand to silence him. "That moment I fell from happiness to despair. I suffered in an instant enough for a lifetime. It was only an hour after that I accepted Mr. Smith as I would have done a pistol bullet."

She paused a moment, closing her red lips tightly, for awakened memory seared a scarce healed wound. The file was still dogmatizing, waving her hands, the fossils gaping it in, nudging, squeaking with satisfaction.

Mrs. T. Tompkins Smith continued : "No, Fred, I did not pine away, allow the worm to feed upon the damask of my cheek, and all that. I love life as I think people of flesh, blood, thews and sinews do, and I shall probably succeed in staggering through what there is left to me of it with fair success, as the world goes. But that night, Fred, all the light went out of it, and since then it has been of the treadmill order."

The man had listened, bent over, his eyes fixed upon the floor. She could scarce see his face, but he bit his mustache, and his bronzed, powerful fingers twisted one into the other as if in pain. He was silent for a while, and then looked up.

"It is all gone by now, Margaret," he said slowly, like a man wearied of a long race, "and regrets are useless. We must live out our lives on the lines that we ourselves have unwittingly marked out, or perhaps a mischievous fate has marked for us. It's just as well I should tell you what you saw. It may now do a little good that we should part with a better opinion of each other. There was fault of mine in that episode, though, God knows, no meant lack of fealty to you."

He stopped, for the train was slowing up for a way station in the desert, and when it stood still a dozen brown and dirty hands, eloquent in beggary, were thrust up to the open window at which he sat, and as many voices whined : "Un centavito, señor ; por Dios, señorita, un centavito."

Angered at the interruption, he sent them to the devil in good Spanish ; but some one of them had recognized him, and the lazzaroni exploded in a series of "Viva Don Federico !" He stopped their mouths with a handful of silver cast among them, and then the train drew on again.

"You see," he resumed in the same tone, when the wheels had gathered headway enough to drown his voice from itching ears, "I met Nellie Stanhope two years before I knew you. It was one of those liaisons a man in society drifts into somehow, and then is too weak or does not know how to get out of. So it went along till I met you. Well, you see you were the only love of my life, too, Margaret, and it did not take me long to tell her that she and I must part. I suppose I talked a deal of rot to the poor woman about her future and her husband, and all that, for which I ought to have been horsewhipped; but I did not realize it then, and said the only thing that occurred to me, not wishing to madden her by telling her I cared for someone else. She took it, though, and I did not see her again for many months until the night of Van Steen's ball. Then she cornered me in the alcove and cursed me for half an hour, threatening to scream and cause a scandal if I left. Suddenly she turned, threw both arms around my neck, and kissed me. Now that I know you were there, I think she saw you and

did it purposely. I left her, however, imme-
diately, and sought you everywhere ; finally,
they told me you had gone home with your
mother and Tom Smith. The next morning
I got your letter. I could not stay in New
York any longer, so turned into money what
little I had, pulled up stakes and came out here,
where I have realized the French proverb, *mal-
heureux en amour, heureux au jeu.*"

He stopped. They understood each other
now. The story was older than the pyramids.
She knew he spoke the truth. Her fingers,
clasped about the arm of the seat, sank into the
velvet, and two tears, starting from the blue
eyes, rolled slowly down her cheeks and fell
upon her other hand that lay upon her knee. The
man knocked a book from the seat beside him
to the floor, and stooping low to pick it up,
pressed his lips to this hand. She did not draw
it away, rather pushed it to him. 'Twas little
enough, that kiss.

A moment later Mr. T. Tompkins Smith and

Mr. Jarr came out of the smoking-room, and the surprise of the former was not small when he saw his wife in deep converse with the man in Mexican dress.

Introductions solved the puzzle.

" My husband—Mr. Frederick Hawthorne, an old friend of mine, formerly of New York.　Mr. Jarr—Mr. Hawthorne."

The men shook hands, Mr. Smith very cordially.

" Why, of course I remember you.　Fuller & Hawthorne, on Broad Street.　Fuller was a member of the Exchange.　Poor fellow, went down with Hutch's grain corner last year.　Glad to see you again.　How long have you been down here ?"

Hawthorne entered easily into explanations. Told of his lucky strike in the Sierra Mojada. Bought out a worthless mine for a song and struck pay ore three days afterward, two hundred ounces silver to the ton.　Yes, lead ores, of course.　Got into this railroad in the subcellar, and turned over his share of the deal while the boom lasted.   And so on.   Made something out of it.

T. Tompkins Smith's eyes glistened ; he struck his knee with the palm of his hand in emphatic approval.   Mr. Jarr smiled, much interested. The woman looked at the speaker, fascinated, thinking, hearing little of what he said.   He was to her as some bronzed giant, telling of battles with Titans, these conquered.   Would she had stood with him, bearing the brunt !   (Some woman had, probably, for the time.)   She was conscious of pain now.   Bah !   Why worry over the past, irrevocable ?   The blood started again, coursing more quickly, flaming.   How lucky people cannot read your thoughts.   Do other women think such things ? .   .   .

The conductor traversed and interrupted, just as the air-brakes were throttling the wheels, "Excuse me, dinner station.   We stop here thirty minutes."

The station baked in a glare of heat.   They

alighted from the car, Don Federico helping Mrs. Smith, and entered the sultry dining-room. He had telegraphed ahead, as usual, for a special dinner, and dividing it with the others, these fared less badly than otherwise they would have done. Two bottles of Don Federico's wine, from the private stock kept for him by the station master, filled the measure of T. Tompkins Smith's happiness to the brim. The worthy stock broker held the ruby-colored Lafitte to the light, smelled it, tasted it reverently. "You couldn't buy this in New York for money," he exclaimed, oracularly. Then turning to Don Federico and holding up his glass : "What is it the Mexicans say ?   Salood ?"

"Salud." Don Federico bowed and emptied his glass. Mr. Jarr remarked that he never could get that soft sound of the Spanish final "d," though he could speak the language well enough to get along. Mrs. Smith had a fair knowledge of French and German, but wished she knew Spanish—had heard there were some exquisite things in modern Spanish literature. A friend of hers had told her that Emilia Pardo Bazan was the greatest living woman writer.

The conductor again, smiling and wiping his mouth : "Don't hurry, ladies and gentlemen ; plenty of time."

The meal over, they strolled out upon the platform, instantly surrounded by beggars, pleading, importunate, bravadoing hideous deformities. Mrs. Smith, shuddering, peremptorily ordered her husband to give a silver dollar to a hag clad in a remnant of calico, holding a shrunken child to shrunken breasts. He complied, grumbling : "If these people would only work—"

"What at ?" snapped Don Federico.

A correct answer would have solved a question bothering the statesmen of the country, but T. Tompkins Smith did not give it, for just at that moment the bell of the engine rang out, and the passengers hurried to board the train.

"These people have souls," whispered Don

Federico to Mrs. Smith, as he assisted her up the steps.

"A woman with a child must have a soul," she replied, adding doubtfully, "if any of us have."

They together chatted the afternoon away with all subjects, from Carlyle to coffee plantations in Tamaulipas. Later, when the sun was slanting its rays across the desert, the train stopped at a section house rather longer than seemed needful. T. Tompkins Smith, curious and aching for movement, left his companions and went forward.

"What are we waiting for?" he queried of the oily and grimy being who ran the engine.

"Water," was the laconic answer.

A cigar, tendered by the questioner, loosened the grimy being's tongue.

"You see, the tank car busted, sprung a leak, and when we tried to pump into the engine there warn't nothin' there. Left it on the road, I reckon. Have telegraphed on ahead for another tank car." He reckoned, too, that it would be a couple of hours before the water would reach them. Smith hurried back to communicate the news to his companions.

" Would you like to take a stroll over the desert ? It's much cooler now than it was." Don Federico bent over Mrs. Smith, pleading with tongue and eyes, regardless of ownership. She assented, adjusting her hat before the mirror, giving it a little touch here and there, deftly. Then she arose and followed him. When they were out of ear shot he turned to her suddenly :

" I am going back to New York next month."

She lifted her blue eyes to his, searchingly.

" What for ? "

" To be near you. Listen, Margaret. Until I met you again I thought I could go through life without you. Now I know I can't. I have been much alone in the last few years, alone in mountain, plain, and desert. If solitude teaches a man anything, it teaches him the power of will.

How foolishly we mar our own lives, Margaret, when it lies in us to do otherwise! You and I could sit down like two children crying over a broken toy, or, if we would, make our future lives as glorious as those of gods! Which shall it be, Margaret?"

She was looking at the distant mountain peaks that broke the coast line to the south.

"I was thinking, Fred, of that beautiful little poem of Heine's that you and I tried to put into good English once, in the old days, and failed. Do you remember it?" She quoted, the German in her sweet mouth sounding soft as Spanish:

" Ein Fichtenbaum steht einsam
    Im Norden auf kahler Höhe.
    Ihn schläfert; mit weiszer Decke
    Umhüllen ihn Eis und Schnee.

" Er träumt von einer Palme,
    Die fern im Morgenland
    Einsam und schweigend trauert
    Auf brennender Felsenwand."

Ere she completed the lines the man had shrugged his shoulders impatiently. "That illustrates the very point I wish to make, Margaret. A pine is alone in the North, sleeping and dreaming of a palm that mourns for him in the South; but don't you see they are trees,—or weak people, if you like. If that pine had the power of locomotion, don't you see that he'd be a fool to stay up there in the North, sleeping in the cold and ice, instead of coming South and getting the palm?"

She laughed softly at his vehemence.

"Don't *you* see that other things besides the mere lack of power to move may have kept the pine fixed in the frozen earth? It is more than probable that Heine thought of those other things when he wrote the poem. Look at those two sharp peaks." She pointed to the distant mountains, purpling in the setting sun. "They ought to be called the twins, they are so exactly alike, yet there they have stood for ages and will always stand, unable to approach each other,

though they may yearn to do so to heartbreak-
ing, as the pine yearned for the palm. When
those peaks are joined, Fred, then may we be."

Her voice trembled in spite of her efforts. She
felt like a person writing his own epitaph, closing from within the only outlet of his vault
where through leapt the glad sunshine.

They stood silent for a while, as the soft eventide fell upon the plain. Suddenly the man
seized the woman's arm in a grip like that of an
iron vise. He quivered with excitement; he
shouted like a Viking at sea:

"Look! look! By Heaven, a miracle! A
sign! A portent! Margaret, the peaks are
joined!"

Yes, one of the many clouds, round and fleecy
as fat sheep, that had been floating lazily across
the heavens, had struck the western peak and
stopped for a moment; then, little by little, this
cloud lengthened out till it met the eastern peak,
forming a bridge between the two.

She looked doubtingly, scarce believing what

she saw; then, half conquered, turned upon him the pleading look of a trapped animal. There was in her a bit of inherited superstition, as there is in the best of us, and to her this phenomenon was almost miraculous. Not so to him, for he had seen it often in the mountains that rise from the high tableland — but that it should occur just then! A coincidence?

Pleading, yet loving, she looked at him. Ah! he would have given his silver mine in the Sierra Mojada twice over to have taken her in his arms then and there and kissed her tempting, trembling mouth; but not half a mile away was the train, and T. Tompkins Smith and Mr. Jarr, to say nothing of the file and the fossils, and not foliage enough betwixt Don Federico and all these to hide a jack rabbit. The desert was a good chaperon.

Don Federico and his companion turned and walked back in silence. He feared to say more, lest he should provoke opposition, preferring to hope on the half consent he had wrung from her.

9

As they neared the train Smith's voice rang out : "Did you see that cloud on the mountains ? Wasn't it funny ?"

Don Federico acknowledged that it was, and Mr. Jarr added something about a bridge for the gods to march into Valhalla, whereupon Mr. Smith asked him if that were in Mexico.

Just then a black speck appeared upon the horizon, where the converging lines of steel met, and a shrill shriek tore through the purple air. The tank car was coming, so the passengers hastened back to the sleeper, where the negro porter was already beginning to make up the beds.

Mrs. T. Tompkins Smith, heedless of supper to come, and pretexting headache, withdrew behind the curtains of her section, and, partially disrobing, threw herself upon the bed.

Her mind was in a whirl ; the events of the day had thrown her from her moral balance. She must be alone, to smooth out the wrinkled, crumpled sheet of the past and read it clearly.

Her emotions must be dominated, thrust back into their respective places, weighed and analyzed ; shadow and substance, fireflies and comets, distinguished. She was playing a game with her future for the stakes, and it behooved her to look well to the cards. Two ways were open to her—the narrow path, leading through New York society, to T. Tompkins Smith ; the broad one, through the desert, to Don Federico. She looked back over seven years, and they were as the seven lean kine, seven pallid milestones on a dull and dusky road. And the future, ay de mi ! She could hear in advance the weary hours rung out by a wearied clock, ticking her, leaden footed, into eternity—with T. Tompkins Smith. To have striven along this path with anything like equanimity she must have felt quite sure of the priest-promised prize at the end of it all, and somehow, in the garish light of the end of the century, she didn't. And the other way ! Now that she had seen again the lover of her youth, every fibre of her being strove toward

him, every beat of her heart sounded his name.
With him the path would be pink-rose strewn,
made merry with the melody of affinity—even if
it were but for a day, with door-closing (or door-
opening ?) death at the end of it.   But duty !
She could hear the clank, clank, clank, as the
wheels leapt from rail to rail.   Whirr !   A score
of skeletons danced about her, dirging in chorus:
"Duty, duty, duty !"   Now they spun round
and round like whirling dervishes, drawing ever
nearer to her, till they seemed about to lay their
clammy hands upon her, and she would have
shrieked in her affright when there rose a tall
form, at the sight of which the skeletons vanished.   The appearance was shrouded from neck
to foot in misty white.   The face was indistinct
but for two balls of fire that stood for eyes,
and seemed to compass her about with flame.
She felt herself giving, yielding, melting, and the
next moment she knew nothing, for she was
sound asleep.

Don Federico sat the night out on the rear

platform of the Pullman, looking up into the black, spangled infinity, and out upon the hilled desert full of strange shadows. His purpose was a single arrow gathered into the bow of his will, drawn taut. It seemed to him that he could see her lying there in her bed behind the curtains, one white arm above her head, her eyes closed in sleep. His force penetrated, wrapped, and swayed her; she quivered under it like a wounded thing. He would carry off the woman he loved, like a Berserker. Fight if need be, and glory in it. He would crush her, tenderly, lovingly. The strong win, the weak lose; he had learned that in the desert. *He* would win. His muscles itched for the combat. . . . How slow were the stars in moving out the night!

The day came, and most of it passed with the trite on the surface, two torrents roaring beneath; T. Tompkins Smith gay with telegraphic news of a rise in stocks, flung out from a way station.

They had left the deserts of the North behind them, wheeling into fields of maguey; cool and blue acequias framed in bright green; adobe huts from whose low doors peered brown women, curious of the passing train. Men in peaked hats, sullen faced, muttered curses upon the iron horse of the Gringos, which sped by like a comet, tailing a cloud of yellow dust that pricked their nostrils. Dinner at six, very good, at a spacious stone station. Mr. Jarr insisted upon opening a couple of bottles of champagne to celebrate things in general and their future happiness in particular. T. Tompkins Smith grew facetious, told some good stories, dropping his voice at passages that were a bit off color, and they all laughed loudly, a strain in the laughter of two, taut to breaking.

The file and the fossils at another table, peering, were properly shocked. *Them* New Yorkers! A contempt that wheezed and sniffed.

After dinner Mr. Smith and his friend Mr. Jarr

adjourned to the smoking compartment, digesting, in blue clouds, more good stories to come, Mr. Jarr the victim.

The sun fell down behind the Sierra, and trees and huts whirled by, blurred in the gathering shadows, vanishing finally into black.

Don Federico and Mrs. Tompkins Smith sat together, silent, she straining her eyes out into the void, he watching her, intent.   In a moment he would throw the dice—Quien sabe?

The locomotive shrieked out into the night, the bell clanged, the brakes pressed heavily upon the wheels.

Don Federico glanced at his watch, looked around the empty car, and then bending over, in a voice that was hard as steel and unwavering as death, said to the woman who sat beside him:

"Listen, Margaret.   In a minute we will be at the station where I get off.   I have telegraphed ahead and my man will be there with two horses.   You are mine, and you must come with me.   *Must!*"

She looked up at him, startled, quivering, her face white to the lips.

"Oh! No! Fred, no!" Her voice was a wavering wail.

His eyes glistened. "You must, Margaret," he repeated, in a low, firm voice; "you will come with me to the old hacienda on the crags, a night's gallop from here, and there we will live our lives out together."

The train was slowing up.

"Come!" She half rose from her seat at the command.

The train had stopped now.

"Come!" He led the way to the rear end of the Pullman. She followed, protesting: "Oh! Fred, please! This is cowardly."

They were out on the platform. He lifted her to the ground, and, taking her by the arm, hurried on, passing quickly the zone of light that fell from the car windows, and then into the darkness beyond. "Please, Fred, let me go," she pleaded, in a low tone.

He laughed softly, but hastened on.

"Let *you* go, Margaret? Never!"

He half lifted her over some stones that would have bruised her feet. She heard the engine whistle, and then the train rolled away to the south, a moving line of light. Don Federico called out: "Antonio!"

A voice came out of the night:

"Aqui! Señor."

"Are the horses there?"

"Aqui estan, Señor."

Now they could hear stamping hoofs.

"Fred!" A last appeal.

His answer was to catch her up in his arms and swing her into the saddle. He leapt upon the other horse.

"Antonio!"

"Si, Señor."

"You will stay about here till morning and hear all that is said. Then borrow a horse from Don Gasparo and come straight to the hacienda. Ears open and mouth shut."

"Si, Don Federico, en boca cerrada no entran moscas."

Don Federico leaned over and seized the bridle of Margaret's horse. Huy! The spurs fell upon the animal's flanks and they shot out into the night. Now they were in the open, where the starlight fell unhindered on the plain. Huy! The hoofs rang on the hard earth. Margaret swayed in the ugly, peaked saddle. Don Federico perceived it and forced his horse close to hers, till the sides of the animals touched ; then put his arm about her waist, compelling her to lean against him, gathering both bridles into his other hand. The two horses galloped as one.

"Margaret!"

No answer. He could not see her face. She lay heavily upon him.

"Margaret!"

Still no answer. The man grew pale with fear. "Margaret, speak to me. Darling, I will take you back if you wish it. We can telegraph, and explain that we were left by the train." He faltered ; his voice broke ; his courage was leaving him, now that he had won. "Shall we go back ? " His hand was straining at the bridles.

She turned and lifted her face up to his, a curious little smile trembling upon her lips.

"No," she whispered.

His arm tightened about her, he shouted in triumph, the sound echoing from the gnarled hills like a blast from a clarion.

Above them the snowy summit of the Nevada de Toluca, silvered by the rising moon, gleamed like the crown of a queen.

And the horses swept on, through the night.

The Vision of Don Juan on the Piedra
de los Angeles

"If a man take into his hand one that is yellow, changing into cloud-like gray, and sleep, he will have strange dreams."

The Vision
of
Don Juan
on the Piedra
de los Angeles

THE sound of a horse's gallop echoed clearly from the cañon walls to the cluster of adobe huts which from time immemorial had borne the name of Tlatzmatlapan.

As yet the animal could not be seen, for there was a sharp turn in the cañon ere it debouched, like the mouth of a huge bellows, into the valley; but the clatter awoke from their dreaming the dwellers of the huts, who issued as with one accord from the low doors, and eagerly watched the barranca.

Now a cry rent the air—long, swelling, ending in a hissing quaver—"Vengo con Di-o—sss !"

and all smiled, for they knew 'twas the cry of Pedro the carrier, and that God had been with him during his long ride from the vale of Anahuac. Good Padre Mateo came out from the little capilla where he had been preparing for vespers, and joined the watching group, for there might be a letter from the bishop or the padre's brother in Puebla, quien sabe ?

"Adios, Pedro !" came from a score of throats as the rider turned into view. Without drawing rein, and with brave clinking of chain and spur, he dashed into the centre of the dusty plaza, and then, by a sudden twist of the rope bridle, threw the animal he rode back upon its haunches, himself scarce moving at the shock.

"Mail for Don Juan!" cried Pedro, shaking a leathern bag above his head and looking about him with an air of important inquiry.

At this all hands pointed to a man who lay stretched out in a hammock suspended under a thatched roof. Touching the side of his horse with his spur, Pedro rode up to the recumbent figure, and with a bow handed the leathern bag, making another yet lower as the silver pieces given in return clinked in his hand. Then with a "Muchas gracias, Señor," he walked his horse over to where the assembled villagers awaited him, there to retail much of the gossip he had learned in the valley below, upon the smooth plains of Anahuac, where the white City of the Sun lies under the guard of Ixtaccihuatl, the White Woman, first, however, giving to the padre a recent copy of the *Voz de Mexico*, much to the delight of the good man, who loved to read the news of the day in a paper the bishop himself approved of.

Don Juan arose from his hammock, and at the first tinkle of the bell that called to vespers walked up the steep path that led to the Piedra de los Angeles, a rock that jutted abruptly out of the side of Tare-Tzuruan, the highest peak in the State of Michoacan. One could but remark, as he leapt from stone to stone, that the name of Don Juan sat illy upon him. The tall yet massive form, the blond hair and beard, the eyes of deep sea-blue, all told of Viking blood, very different from the Tenorio of poem and story. But then no Mexican tongue could say his uncouth northern name, so he had given the villagers "Don Juan" as a handle of address, and these simple Indian folk were content therewith, the Don distinguishing him from the many other Juans, Juanchos, and Juanitos who lay around.

"See!" cried Pedro the carrier, stopping for a moment his tale of the wondrous fiestas he had seen in the great city, where the President of the Republic had just reëlected himself, and pointing to the mountain side, "there goes Don Juan up the mountain. What can he do there now?"

"Caray," answered old Concha, who, by reason of her age, good memory, and ready tongue, took the lead in village discussion. "He goes to sit on yon rock and smoke of an evening. Why, I know not. Lucky for him he does not sleep there!"

"Why?" queried Pedro.

"Why," repeated the madre, with some contempt in her tone, "hast thou passed here so
many times since the government gave thee thy
place, Pedro, and knowest not that yon rock is
the rock of the angels, and that he who sleeps
a night there never awakens?"

"Why?" again Pedro.

"Carramba! Thou art made of 'whys,' Pedro,"
exclaimed the old woman, stamping her foot
impatiently, yet withal not ill-pleased to have the
tale to tell again. "Well, it is because if one
sleeps there at night the angels come down and
take away his soul."

"Buena historia, esa," replied Pedro, looking
laughingly around and curling his moustache.

"A good story, is it!" shrieked old Concha,
trembling with rage. "The next thing thou wilt
be doubting the holy sacrament and the saints in
paradise! Three times did it occur in the lifetime of my mother, who is with God, and many
a time has she told me the tale. Besides, 'tis all
written down on yellow paper by the cura of

this place, the one we had before Padre Mateo, and with a seal on it as big as my hand! And if thou wilt go up there thou wilt see a cross cut in the stone!"

"'Tis well, madre," interjected Pedro at the first opportunity, desirous of staying the old woman's wrath and torrent of words, but she would not heed him !

"I tell thee, boy, thou art losing thy faith since thou hast been employed by this unholy government of Porfirio Diaz, who respects not the Church nor the ministers of God. Ave Maria purissima, but thou wilt be damned !"

"Hush, madre !" cried a young girl, as with the blood darkening her brown cheek she sprang to the carrier's side. " You go too far. Pedro is no heretic."

The carrier put his arm affectionately about the girl's waist. " All here know that as soon as the rainy season begins, Conchita and I marry, and she goes with me to the city to live. She will have a hat with flowers and feathers in it, and walk with me in the Alameda Sunday noon, amidst the best of the caballeros. Is it not so, chiquita ? "

The old woman drew away, mumbling, for she saw that all were with Pedro and against her ; but her wrath knew no limit when any one doubted the story of the holy stone that thrust itself so strangely and abruptly from the smooth side of gigantic Tare-Tzuruan.

In the meantime Don Juan had reached the rock, followed by a little yellow dog that kept close to his heels. Seating himself and lighting a Victoria de Colon, he untied the thong that closed the bag and shook out a score of letters upon his knees. Carelessly he glanced at their contents and tossed them aside, all but one, which he seized with seeming eagerness. His name was penned upon it as finely as if with the engraver's tool and art, and the postmark bore the name of a city of the North.

He tore open the envelope and slowly read the pink sheet that it had held. When he had finished he laid it aside and took from his pocket the picture of a woman, at which he gazed long and attentively ; then he took letter and picture, and throwing them upon the rock, ground them to powder with his heel, not angrily, but rather as if weary, utterly weary of it all.

Drawing his zarape more closely about him, he lay back, resting his head upon his hand, and watched the sun fall behind the ragged Sierra, outlining it in fire. Out of bottomless barrancas and yawning holes dug by gold-seekers of old came the black shadows, creeping out into the valley, stealing up the mountain sides till they reached and quenched the glow that still lingered upon the peaks. The stars glittered out of the dark canopy above, and a cold wind moaned down the cañon. Still Don Juan did not move, but gazed steadily into space, and the yellow dog nestled closer to him.

From the village below came the notes of old Tiburcio's violin and the clamor of singing

women, filtered by the heavy air into a single
chord of harmony.   Still Don Juan gazed steadily
out upon the blackness and the void ; for memory, that tricky painter of mingled truth and lie,
was making for him a multicolored phantasm,
toned throughout with the misty gray of non-
fruition.   The picture grew duller, the figures
blending shadow-fashion into grotesquerie, and
he became keener to the sounds without, the
voices of the night, deep monotones cut athwart
by sharp cry of bird or beast.   The stars shone
with a swifter light, marking deeper their setting of infinity ; but one, that hung just above
a spear-like peak, even as the dot upon an
"i," sent a luminous shaft, clear and distinct, to
the very rock whereon lay Don Juan.

Scarce had he time to note this, when he saw
a figure coming down this glittering pathway, a
figure of shining haze, yet well marked in form
and feature.   Another followed, and another,
until six in all moved toward him.   What
strange phantasm was this ?   He sat up that he

might see more surely, and the yellow dog by his side moaned and hid its face in a fold of its master's zarape.

The first of the throng placed a foot upon the rock, and passed him so closely that he might have touched her with his hand. It was a woman, one he had well known in years gone by. Well he knew the stately form and proud face, the eyes which, though cold to all others, had softened to him—only for a moment. Her pride pricked her for a fall. But he felt no regret that it was bygone, and had for greeting to her but a smile, hinting at contempt. Slowly this figure vanished, seemingly adown the mountain side, engulfed, and the next strode before him. She held in one hand a bunch of scarlet flowers, and in the other a cup of wine which her joyous laugh spiced with the hope of pleasures to come, keen to rending. Her dark eyes and red lips spoke of love, and her rounded limbs, and men had given gold and honor that they might touch her hair. Well he knew her, too. She had come into his life and gone out of it, a dream without dregs, and he smiled, as she passed on, a smile of pleased remembrance.

Then came one of slender form and anguished countenance, as of one who had sinned and was sorely troubled thereat, beating her breast that memories of pleasant hours might not rise and stand 'twixt her and soul's salvation ; her eyes were heavy with reproach and querulous repining. He laughed mockingly as she moved away.

There stepped behind her a girl of dull form, but flecked sharp with bright color of flower and feather and gleaming jewel. Though featured, her face was a blank whereon petty vices and weakly virtues writhed and marked themselves like dun serpents, drugged, slow moving to a dim and feeble piping. The pride in her step was from numbers ; for could she have waved her hand and evoked her like throughout the world's broad plains, the heavens would have blackened with the rising myriad.

Don Juan turned wearily from her to the one

who followed.   Here was force—force in the lithe and supple form, force in the dark eyes that flashed anger and revenge, force in the nervous fingers that clutched the hilt of a shadowy knife and yearned to plunge it into the breast of the man who lay upon the rock.   She struggled to reach him, and when borne on by some invisible power, she shrieked, baffled—no, 'twas only the cry of some night bird caught in the cañon.

But now the way that lay from the star grew brighter, and adown it came two figures, a woman and child, at the sight of whom Don Juan rose to a sitting posture and his breath came quick and sharp.   The woman's brown hair fell about her like a veil, framing a pallid face whereon was writ infinite sadness and the suffering that is not to end through all the roll of centuries, not even when the earth splits asunder and falls screaming through space.   Both hands of the fair-haired child were clasped to one of hers, and its blue eyes looked up to her darker ones with trusting worship.   She saw the man upon the rock, but in her look was naught of reproach nor of complaining, only tenderness without bounds. Don Juan moaned in his pain, and sank his nails into his breast until red drops followed the cut. Then he held out his hands to her, imploring ; but she, understanding, gently shook her head. Love such as hers would have only what it gave, and she well knew that this would never come to Don Juan, and he suffered that he could not create it. The boundaries of fate are higher than the stars and stronger than the ages, and she blamed not him that he could not love, but the Parcæ, who twisted the threads of life, or ran them singly through the ever-moving shuttle. She bowed to the decree of the Fates ; he would have struggled against it, though knowing such struggle to be vain. He held out his hands to her, but even as he did so the figures grew misty, and soon where they stood was but the black sheath of the night, jewelled with quiet stars.

The man, bending over, hid his face in his

hands, and the yellow dog thrust its head out from the folds of the zarape and licked the hands softly.

The night sped on, and now the deep silence seemed to vibrate, at first into a low monotone, rising higher until it broke into a cadence of softer notes, the harmony of the whirling atoms in rock and tree and tinkling water. Don Juan listened, and this harmony broke into words, a voice distinctly speaking:

"Over, over, over the waters I move, o'er broad plain and peakèd hill. He who lays o'er night upon this rock will see the past and know the future. Look up, Don Juan."

The musical syllables were loud and clear, seemingly at his side, and he took his hands from his face and looked up.

Beside him stood a form of perfect beauty, such as in the sculptor's dream floats above the hired model when the artist, despairing, lets fall his chisel, clanging upon the marble. He marvelled at her beauty, and yet more at her words.

Never had he seen her; no hidden door of memory opened as he gazed upon her. He felt within him a sense of peace, of quiet infinite, that recked not of the fall of worlds, that soothed the pain in his breast, and healed all wounds as though they had never been. She bent over and placed her hand upon his brow.

"Thou hast sought love, Don Juan, and found it not. Evil hast thou wrought, seeking it, but for this blame the Fates, not thyself, for they led thee winding ways. This much may I tell thee; that before thou reachest the end thou wilt meet me, and thou shalt know love as the gods know it, eternal and infinite. We two have sought each other through the ages, ever since the soul was born of the first woman who sorrowed in love, and it is written that we shall meet. So be of good cheer and journey on, fearing not, and I await thee." She bent over him till her lips were upon his. Her kiss thrilled him like the touch of a god. He put out his arms to enfold her—but there was nothing there. Still he could hear the music of the voice : "Over, over, over the waters I go, o'er broad plain and peakèd hill. . . ." The voice sank into a monotone, and this dwindled into silence again, and Don Juan slept, his head upon his arm, the yellow dog shivering in the folds of its master's zarape.

Tap! Tap! Tap! "Padre Mateo! Padre mio, for the love of God come quickly!" 'Twas the voice of old Concha, standing without, and at the sound of it the priest arose from his couch and went to his door. "What is it, my daughter?" he called from within.

"Ave Maria, Padre," she whispered shrilly, " but Don Juan the Americano has gone to sleep on the Stone of the Angels, and they are taking away his soul !"

Quickly the padre threw about him his new black robe, over this a blanket, and thrusting his feet into his sandals opened the door and hurried out upon the plaza. He saw there the entire population of Tlatzmatlapan huddled together and shivering, their blankets drawn about them, covering their faces up to their eyes.

Old Concha seized the priest's arm as he came out. "Look," she whispered, pointing to the Piedra de los Angeles on the side of mighty Tare-Tzuruan. "I saw that Don Juan did not come back, and I watched the rock, and but a moment ago I saw a light upon it. Ave Maria purissima! See!"

The padre gazed steadily, his arm still held by the old woman. Perhaps in some corner of his nature there had lurked a doubt as to the legend so carefully cherished in the records of his church, but now, by Our Lady of Guadalupe! there could be none, for he saw it with his own eyes—and if you cannot trust them, what can you trust, eh? Juan Diego himself, when he saw the miraculous Virgin on the hill of Guadalupe, had nothing but his eyes to see with. The new doctrine of contagious hallucination had not yet found its way to far Tlatzmatlapan, and if it had, the good padre would rather trust to the eyes that God had given him than to the ridiculous theories of a parcel of heretical Frenchmen. He *saw* it; *saw* the stone lit up with a strange light that was like nothing ever seen of this earth, and forms of flame moving therein. After a while, one greater, more brilliant than the rest —then all vanished, and darkness again shrouded the holy stone.

A long time thereafter the watchers were silent, only breaking out now and then into a whispered Ave Maria or a Nuestro Señor, for a great awe was upon them. Had there been devils on yonder rock there is no doubt the padre, armed with a crucifix and a bowl of holy water, would have marched straight to the rescue, for he was a man of kindly impulse and withal brave enough in his way. But with angels one must bow to the will of God.

So they stood there the night through, waiting until the first arrow of Tonatiuh tipped with gold the peak of Tare-Tzuruan and drove away the spirits of darkness, giving courage to the hearts of those whose forefathers had worshipped him.

Now, at a nod from the priest, Pedro the carrier and José the sacristan went together to the church and got therefrom the stretcher of wood and leather that had served to carry many to their last rest in the Campo Santo. As a heretic, Don Juan could scarce be buried there in holy ground, but if the angels had taken his soul, carramba! 'twas a case over which the archbishop himself might well puzzle and lose his Latin. But they could bring him down from yon rock, and then—to-morrow they would decide what to do.

So a procession was formed and started bravely up the path. First the padre, with a crucifix, for one never could be *quite* sure about angels when heretics were in question. Then Pedro and José carrying the stretcher. Next, Madre Concha, fairly bursting with pride and piety, her faded blue rebozo drawn tightly over head and shoulders. The entire population followed,

11

even to the chicos, clinging fearfully to their mothers' skirts.

Up the steep path they wound till just beneath the rock, beyond the edge of which projected a man's boot and the sharp nose of a little yellow dog.   Here   the   padre   stopped   a   moment, doubtless for breath, and the rest did likewise. The little yellow dog eyed them doubtfully.   It was not quite sure of their intentions.   Two or three times it opened its mouth as if to bark, then shut it again to await further developments. The padre started, winding around the rock, and now was upon it.   There lay Don Juan, as large as life, stretched out upon the hard stone, his head resting upon his arm, his bright-hued zarape wound about him.   At this juncture the yellow dog came to a decision, and opening widely its mouth, emitted a sharp, clear yelp which cut the air like a knife, and then the body on the rock *moved*.

The footing of Padre Mateo upon the steep side was at best precarious, and by a coincidence he lost his equilibrium at this particular moment, falling heavily against Pedro, who in turn jammed the stretcher into José, who knocked down Madre Concha, and the next instant all these good people were rolling down the mountain side in a confused heap, amid the cries of terror of the villagers. 'Twas not long, however, ere they stopped, unmixed themselves unharmed, and the padre, angry with himself, bounded up to the rock. He was just in time to see the recumbent figure stretch out an arm, then a leg, open its mouth in an abysmal yawn, and sit up.

"You are alive and well, Señor?" cried the padre in something of a strangled voice.

"I think so," replied Don Juan in a natural but sleepy tone, gazing with some wonderment at the awed and astonished faces of those who now crowded the narrow platform.

"But the angels, Señor?" cried Concha, in mingled wrath and disappointment ; "hast thou seen no angels this night?"

Don Juan passed his hand over his forehead.

"Yes, angels and devils, madrecita. I have dreamed strange dreams upon your rock, for a truth. But," he added, coming fully to himself and catching sight of the stretcher which José and Pedro were making desperate efforts to hide, "I do not need that yet, my friends!" and he leapt to his feet, in his full strength, and the yellow dog executed a fantastic joy-dance about his heels.

Respectfully they made way for him to pass down. As he came to Conchita, who clung fearfully to Pedro's arm, he drew from his finger a ring. "Take this, girl, as a wedding present from the man who slept on the Piedra de los Angeles, and may it bring thee luck and love. And you, José," he added, turning to the sacristan, "saddle my horse quickly, for after a tortilla and a cup of the madrecita's coffee, I go down to Anahuac."

He strode on down the mountain, the rest following slowly in whispering groups.

That morning he rode out along the cañon, after many farewells and " Vaya Vd. con Dios " from these simple folk. At first he let the rein hang idly over the high peak of his Mexican saddle, the horse picking its way as it would, the man lost in thought.

Was, then, all this true ? Was there before him, in what was left to him of life, the perfect woman, the love that knows not doubt nor sorrow, that makes gods of men ?

But a moment later he seized the reins and drove his spurs into the flanks of his horse.

He did not believe it.

Cosmopolitana Mexicana

"And a handful of divers hues, which may mean anything or nothing, as one will."

Cosmopolitana
Mexicana

Jornada I

IT was a great holiday, the Saturday following Good Friday, and the city was in gala dress. To one who knows the climate of Mexico, some eight thousand feet nearer the clouds than sea-coast towns, it is needless to add that the weather was fine, the sky unflecked by a cloud, the sun dazzling. Eight months of clear, bright days, one so like unto the other that you long for a tempest and thirst for a patter of rain, wishing the sun moon-like, with quarters. Now, even about the forehead, breasts, and knees of the White Woman, Ixtaccihuatl, there was no crown nor wreath of mist, nor a bit of smoke lingering about the cones of Popocatepetl. Only one great expanse of blue into which the white volcanoes dipped.

In every street, suspended from cords stretched from house to house, were huge dolls, man-size, fantastically painted and dressed, the Judases which were to be this day shot, knifed, and burned, that the people might thus fittingly show their hatred of the one who had betrayed the gentle Christ.

The Zocalo, the great square in front of the cathedral, swarmed with a multicolored mass of humanity, pushing and jostling good naturedly, the upper classes in sombre black and gray, the lower in zarapes of every hue that light contains, and many that it doesn't. Mingling with all were Indian hawkers and peddlers, proffering their wares with shrill cries ; children lugging grotesque dolls to burn at home. Beggars whined and squeaked, dark-skinned women in blue rebozos, from the floating gardens of La Vega, tendered their bouquets of fragrant flowers, while now and then a carriage split the crowd, the driver shouting for way. It was all bathed in splendid sunshine, and splendid music from the military band that played in the kiosk, and deep waves of harmony that rolled out from the great bells swinging in the tall twin towers of the church.

From the plaza the mass flowed into the narrow streets of Plateros and San Francisco, toward the Alameda, for it was near noon, and the fashion and beauty of Mexico must be in the green and shady walks by that hour, to see and be seen, to smile, gossip, and smirk.

In front of the arched door of the palace that was of Iturbide, now fallen to the base uses of a hostelry, stood two degenerate descendants of Aztec kings, clad in peaked straw hats and ragged cotton shirts, holding out their hands, upon every finger of which was perched a live tropical bird of brilliant plumage, seemingly well content and undisturbed by the passing crowd. "Pajaros, pajaritos bonitos, mansos," shrilled the natives in chorus, thrusting the birds almost into the face of every one who bore the marks of a tourist.

"Oh, Dick ! just look at those lovely tame birds," cried a young American woman who hung upon the arm of a young American man, and the demeanor of those two proclaimed to who would read, that they were inseparably, indissolubly, inextricably, and by due process of law, linked in wedlock.

" Ask him how much they are, Dick, do ! "

Dick brought his entire knowledge of the language to bear upon the natives, and uttered the one word, "Cuanto ?"

" Dos pesos, Señor," replied the vendor of birds.

"I guess that means two dollars, Dolly," doubtfully.

"Oh, that's only Mexican dollars, Dick ! " Her eyes yearned to the little feathered bunches.

A tall man who had been standing near her bent over. " Excuse me, madam," he said, "I would advise you not to buy those birds. They have been recently snared in the forests of the Tierra caliente, and a half ounce of small shot has been forced down their throats. This is why they are unable to fly. To-morrow they will be dead ! "

" Oh, dear ! how awfully cruel ! " exclaimed the woman ; and then she and her lawful spouse turned away and were swallowed up in the moving throng.

The tall man gazed for a moment after his countrywoman, who had failed to even nod an appreciation of his courtesy in saving her both expense and trouble. He was not surprised. In her fade but rather pretty face there was no spark of intelligence nor breeding. She was of a certain schoolgirl type, celebrated in song and story, carefully avoided by all wise men.

He was still looking, lost in thought, when a hand was laid upon his arm, and a voice beside him said : " Tiens, c'est toi. Georges ! Justement je te cherchais."

" Ah! Paul," replied the one thus addressed, in

French that bore no trace of being spoken by a Saxon, "I was about to look you up in the Alameda."

"I hope you have no engagement for to-day," continued the Frenchman, vivaciously ; "we will meet Calvo and Petroffski there, and I have ordered dinner at the Café de Paris for one o'clock. They have just received some fresh oysters via Vera Cruz, and I am sick of the table d'hôte at the Jockey Club. Si le cœur t'en dit ?"

The American nodded in acquiescence. Paul chattered on.

"Quel trou, ce Mexique, mon cher, quelle galère, quelle infamie ! It is a most marvellous thing that France should think of keeping a minister or even a chargé d'affaires here. Va pour le ministre ! He seems to like it, but wherefore an attaché ? My poor mother is working night and day to get me out of here and sent to Japan, Tonquin, Tunis, the devil—anywhere. She even went to Clemental,—just think of it, Clemental, —who has such a pull with the ministry that he

was able to send a mari importun to Denmark.
But nothing, nothing. The Deschanteaux are
not in favor with the bourgeois government."

In front of the Jockey Club they were stopped,
the multitude in front of them closing up into a
compact mass. From somewhere beyond came
shouts and cries mingled with laughter.

Paul Deschanteaux tip-toed in vain endeavor
to look over the heads of those in front of him.

"What is it, Georges ?" he finally asked of his
taller companion.

"They're burning Judases in front of the
Jockey Club," replied the American, "and some
of the members are throwing silver to the crowd
from the balcony."

Deciding, after a few vain efforts to push
through, that they would be detained too long,
the two friends backed out of the crowd and
turned into the Calle de Gante, alone now in this
broad street, the murmur behind them growing
fainter. They turned the block, coming out at
the entrance of the main alley of the Alameda,

lined with chairs and covered from the sun, people swarming therein, and the military band at the farther end rolling down full notes, a sonorous background to the cackle and laughter of the throng.   The men in black frock coats, light trousers, French silk hats, shamming gravity. The women in French gowns or home-made imitations, sparkling with feather, flower, and jewel ; the graceful rebozo long since démodé, and relegated to the back stairs.

The two nodded gayly to passing acquaintances.   '' Adios, Don Jaime."   '' Como, Pedro ? '' '' Buenos dias, Don Tiburcio."   These were the limit of Deschanteaux' Spanish—like all his countrymen he was above learning any language other than his own, excepting under circumstances of great provocation.

A group of notaries passed, sedate, and there was a great lifting of shining silk hats, for it must be remembered that in this town every one knows every one else (that's worth knowing). The Chief Justice of the Supreme Court, walking alone, hands behind his back, buried in thought, carrying the Constitution on his shoulders, and prepared to cheerfully violate its most sacred provisions at the nod of the Executive. He lifted his hat gravely, with a whispered "Señores!"

One of the notaries detached himself from the group, and touching the American on the arm, beckoned him aside. "Any news from New York, Don Jorge?"

"None," replied the American, shaking his head wearily. "I don't think there ever will be, Velasco. The company is bankrupt, and in the present condition of the money market cannot raise another dollar for working capital."

"And what are you going to do, then, pobre amigo mio?" inquired the notary, his round, fat face shining with sympathy.

"Sabe Dios," replied the other. The notary glanced back. "Your friend Deschanteaux is talking with Calvo and the Russian. I won't detain you but a moment. Listen. I have a client, Don Cassio Alvarez, who has a great ha-

12

cienda in Guerrero,—mines, cattle, plantation, everything. His last steward robbed him unmercifully and he has discharged him. He wants an American, one whom he can trust. He pays three hundred pesos, Mexican, a month and ten per cent. of the net. He will be here next week, and I thought of you. Can I mention your name ?"

George Forrest grasped the notary's hand and shook it warmly.

"Thanks, amigo. It would be salvation for me. I will confess to you that I do not know where to give head."

"Es nada," answered the good-humored notary, shrugging away the other's gratitude. "Apropos, there is a rendezvous at the Tivoli de San Cosme to-night. Alberigo, Escandor, and others ; will you come?"

"If possible. Thanks."

"Hasta luego, then."

The two separated, and Forrest walked on to join his companion. He found him in animated converse with Petroffski and Don Calvo. The former, blond-bearded, blue-eyed, the body and hands of a mougik, a touch of sentimentalism somewhere about the face, that struggled to offset the hard shrewdness of the Tartar eyes; a queer mixture of Werther and wolf, with the possibilities of a Tolstoi and the probabilities of a brute.

Don Calvo was a type of the Visigoth run clear, on Spanish ground, of Arabic or Jewish blood, or else harked back in a spasm of atavism. Thickset and long-limbed, with reddish blond hair and moustache, and eyes that shifted from gray to steel blue. He was of good stock, and had his father left him a fortune he would have been a gentleman ; with opportunities he might have been a professional gentleman or a commercial gentleman ; with capital he might have drifted along any of the accepted channels of thievery yclept trade, and been a credit to his country. Lacking these, he had become a society broker, giving you cheerfully the price of anything, from a horse to a girl with dark eyes, and accepting a commission gracefully, as a loan. Always ready to do any one a good turn, on the principle that it deserved another. He was tolerated for his good fellowship, much sought after as a budget of news. Not a scandal but he had it at the tips of his fingers, not a conjugal lapse that he could not conjugate. He was better than a Burke's Peerage, and more truthful, for he could tell the relationship of every man and woman in town to the Devil. They marvelled and mumbled at his memory.

As Forrest drew near, Petroffski hailed him with a grunt that rumbled into a laugh.

"To the rescue, Monsieur Forrest! Deschanteaux is engaged in his usual occupation of damning Mexico with ornamental and original aphorisms that were new and startling at the epoch of the deluge, and Calvo is no match for him."

"And what new evil has my friend Paul discovered in la colonie manquée of Napoleon the Little?"

"Nothing new, mon cher, but my manner of putting it," answered Deschanteaux, turning to Forrest. "The two principal topics of conversation in every European capital are, as you know, politics and women. Here only one man talks politics, presumably with himself, and that is the President. As for women, il n'y en a pas." He snapped his fingers to emphasize the void. "So we are reduced to discussing art and literature, and will ultimately be forced into science and theology. Petroffski is threatening us with Tolstoi, and Calvo is ranting about some fellow by the name of Picon, who it seems wrote novels—in Spanish. Yes, mes amis, two months more of this, and if I ever reach home, and you come to visit me, my address will be Charenton, third cell to the right, main corridor; and then," continued Deschanteaux,—for once started on this topic it was difficult to stop him,—"everybody seems to have the amusing and laudable habit of dying of the typhus. Yesterday, while I was taking my afternoon walk on the Paseo, I met a dozen men whom I knew, who had just died of the typhus——"

"What, their ghosts?" inquired Don Calvo.

"Non, gros beta. I mean each of them had just lost some relative by that charming disease. They were either going to or coming from funerals, having just left their former friend in pigeon-hole number 369. N'est-ce pas que c'est gai, eh?"

Don Calvo stood the chaffing good-naturedly.

"Joking aside, Paul," said Forrest, "Calvo is right about Octavio Picon. I am familiar with almost everything in the way of novels in European literature, but I assure you that no pen has ever drawn a more exquisite picture of a woman than Cristeta in *Dulce y Sabrosa.* Am I not right, Petroffski?"

"You are, Forrest," replied the Russian. "But such women only exist, unfortunately, in the imagination of the novelist. They are poetical myths. Now Tolstoi——"

"Pour l'amour de Dieu, Petroffski, stop Tolstoi!" exclaimed Deschanteaux. "Do you know——"

"Let me tell you, gentlemen," interposed Don Calvo, "I knew a beautiful woman here once——"

"She's dead, of course," interrupted Deschanteaux.

"Yes, but——"

"I knew it," and the irrepressible Frenchman began to hum:

> " Il penchait pour l'amour physique
> Et à Rome, séjour d'ennui,
> Une femme, d'ailleurs phtisique,
> Est morte d'amour pour lui."

"Is that original?" queried Petroffski, when the laughter had subsided.

"Yes—with Charles Baudelaire."

"Seriously, Deschanteaux, can't you be serious a moment?" asked the Mexican, with a tinge of impatience in his tone.

"No, my dear friend, I can't. If I were serious for five consecutive minutes I should certainly catch the typhus. Nothing predisposes one so much to that disease as being serious. Don't try it, my dear fellow; if you value your life don't try it, and don't talk to me about beautiful women. It gives me the nostalgia. I have not seen one since I left Paris——"

"Hush!" exclaimed Don Calvo, in a sharp, sudden whisper to the three who stood facing him. "Don't look around, don't move! In a moment I will show you the most beautiful woman in the world, to say nothing of Mexico. She is seated directly behind you, and you cannot look around now. Let us go over to the American minister and see him a moment, and then we can walk by her."

They looked at the speaker in amazement, scarce believing what he said, yet there was no mistaking his tone. Obediently, and successfully resisting the temptation to look behind them, they went over to where O'Brien Mulcahy, the diplomatic representative of the United

States, his wife and two daughters, sat watching the passing crowd and listening to the
music.

"Tell me, Forrest, are all American ministers
Irish?" inquired Petroffski as they approached
the group.

"Certainly."

"And your President, senators and deputies
too?"

"Yes, all of them." This listlessly, for he
had been wearied by much questioning upon
home topics difficult to explain.

"This domination of the Celtic race over the
Saxon is certainly a curious historical phenomenon," said the Russian, reflectively.

The American minister returned the salute of
the four gentlemen with the diplomatic grace and
dignity he had acquired during his many years'
experience as sheriff in a town in Iowa. His
daughters, healthy, rosy-cheeked girls, bowed
and smiled condescendingly, with a suspicion
in manner, however, of not being intimately

acquainted with their new French gowns, and
as yet unused to foreign ways.

"Had the latest papers yet?" queried the
minister of Forrest. "We've got the other
party on the run, and as sure as you're alive,
at the next election we'll sweep the country!"

Forrest nodded in agreement. He did not care
very much which party swept the country so
long as he was not asked to carry away any of
the dirt, and he was impatient to get away.

"You'll come to our reception Tuesday
night," said Mrs. Mulcahy as they moved away,
"all of you."

"Yes, do," added the minister.

They accepted, all but Deschanteaux, who had
not understood a word of the conversation, and
had been nursing a contemptuous wrath for dip-
lomats who could not speak French.

Under the guidance of Don Calvo they strolled
a short distance up the shady walk, and then
wheeling about, two by two, bore down on the
object of their quest.

It was quite needless for the Mexican to nudge Deschanteaux with his elbow when they arrived in front of the lady. It would have been no hard task to have singled her out from among the twelve thousand virgins of Cologne. As they walked by they had but a single glance, and little time for carping details. Against the background of dark green, sun-sprinkled, they saw a figure in gray, with curve of bust and hip which sculptors would have sought as knights the Holy Grail. A face, calm, pure, majestic, surmounted by a coil of dark brown hair crowned by a simple toque of black velvet, relieved only by a golden spray on one side. The eyes they remembered clearly, two wells of deep blue, fathomless.

To their astonishment Don Calvo lifted his hat to the goddess, whereupon they all followed suit, pleased at custom permitting this obeisance. They walked on, rounding the fountain, and then seized Don Calvo. "You know her, then? It's a king's privilege! Wretch! Who and what is she? Speak, or we'll throw you into the basin. Speak, and we'll give you all we have!"

Don Calvo was in his element. He swelled with pride and expanded with satisfaction. It would not do to yield too quickly, however. He paused for a moment, nodding to a passing acquaintance; and then, with feet spread apart, swung his cane to and fro in his gloved hand. At last, patience of others to breaking point, he quoth sagely, and with a smacking of Sir Oracle, "Have I kept my word, gentlemen?"

The affirmations were as of a well-trained chorus.

"Well, you see it is this way. To begin at the beginning, did you notice the respectable old lady who sat beside her, a foil in yellow? No? I thought not. That was Madame Schreiber, who came here some eight years ago with her husband, an American engineer employed on the National Railroad. He died a year later and his salary died with him. It's a question which death the widow regretted the more. Deciding wisely to live, she opened a boarding-house for Americans, baked them pie with her own hands, and flourished exceedingly. By my advice (I speak modestly, gentlemen) she bought a barro in the Santa Rosalia mine and sold out at the proper time, whereupon she gave up baking pies and took a villa out at Tacubaya. The goddess is her niece, who came from your country" (he nodded to Forrest) "a week or ten days ago. Voila !"

"A niece of Madame Schreiber is indefinite," exclaimed Deschanteaux. "Her name, her lineage ?"

"Her name, Alma Lessing; age, twenty-four; lineage, her father, brother to Madame Schreiber, was a coal miner in Pennsylvania, and married a Hungarian woman,—daughter, sister, or something of another miner."

"And how do you know all this ?" asked Petroffski.

"I called on the old lady the other even-

ing, and she introduced me to la Señorita
Alma and gave m the family history from A
to Z."

"All of which means, en somme," said
Petroffski slowly, "that our friend Don Calvo y
Ramirez is both able and willing to introduce us."

"Certainement."

Deschanteaux glanced down the long line of
seats, and spied the black velvet toque and the
gold spray gleaming in a bit of sunlight.

"Now ?" he questioned.

Don Calvo nodded, and they strolled back to
where the two women were seated, listening to
the music, the younger one watching the passing crowd with the interest of one to whom this
land was new.

Introductions were quickly given. Alma extended her small gray-gloved hand to each, cordially, with a gesture that was grace and
strength. One guessed muscles of iron under
the soft glove and softer skin. She looked
frankly into the eyes of each in turn, not with

the boldness of a woman who knows men too well, nor with that of a woman to whom they will never be known. Rather with the glance of one who is politely curious until the hour comes, then only to leap into flame.

Madame Schreiber, clad in a yellow dress that shrieked, was pleased to make acquaintance of men whom she knew stood well, and she monopolized volubly in bad French, propped up here and there by worse Spanish. Her lungs troubled her so—the rarefied air—she felt she must go to San Antonio as soon as her lease was up in June—her house was at Tacubaya, Villa Dominguez—the first turn to the right after you pass the great gambling hall—always at home evenings, and also afternoons, excepting Wednesday and Saturday, when they drove on the Paseo—she would be glad to have them call, sans cérémonie.

They listened to her, nodding approvingly, with now and then a "mais oui" or a "c'est bien vrai" to emphasize. She was doorkeeper to beauty, and hence worthy of deep regard. She would have rattled on to exhaustion of breath had not a dozen bells each given a single musical note on different keys. "Himmel !" exclaimed Madame Schreiber, rising to her feet. "Es la una. Mon Dieu, we shall just have time to catch the tramcar. We shall be late for dinner. Adios, Señores. Villa Dominguez, first road to the right after you pass the gambling hall."

She trotted away, followed by her niece, who bowed pleasantly to the lowering of silk hats. The younger woman walked with light step, as if moving upon smooth joints of gold, bending rhythmically to the music of flowing life. Her plain gray gown hid her form no more than clear glass. The four watched her until she was lost to view in the surging crowd.

"Bones, flesh, tissue, bathed in blood and air," murmured Petroffski, "and the result is *that!* And yet some men say there is no God !"

Paul Deschanteaux drew a long breath. "Well," he said, "shall we dine?"

Jornada II

A week later the city had resumed its workaday look of moving apathy. Few were on the broad Plaza, these crossing to other points. The red, yellow, and blue wheeled hacks stood in a long line, drivers and horses sleeping. There was buzzing and droning, but no clatter nor clash. The mules dragging the tramcars stepped quietly and lightly, the bells as if muffled. The tall man leaned against the huge iron railing in front of the cathedral, his arms folded, under one of them a book. He was dressed in a dark blue flannel suit, a black felt hat pushed back over a mass of curling hair with a silver line in it here and there. His posture was not one of grace, rather of laziness with a touch of dejection. He was surely deep in thought, for a newsboy had twice yelled

"El Democrata!" and flourished the paper under his very nose, and a brown-faced girl had offered him a bunch of pink roses, only a real, *mire Vd.*, and he had not even so much as blinked at them.

"Good afternoon, Mr. Forrest."

The words roused him, and he looked up. Before him stood the gray figure he had seen in the Alameda seven days before, a gray-gloved hand extended, the deep blue eyes looking straight into his. He took the hand eagerly, reaching after his hat, which threatened to fall backward.

"You look as if the fardel of life were heavy," she said, smiling.

"Neither heavy nor light, Miss Lessing; only an empty cask. One can't fly with it."

"Why not fill it, then, and walk? Your shoulders are broad enough. Only those wish to fly who don't know the earth and its treasures."

"To you life is pleasant?"

"It should be to anyone not in physical pain.
It is just what we make it, after all. To me it
is full of beauty and joys to come. I have faith
in the future."

"I had once," he muttered.

She placed her hand upon his arm. "Only
God has the right to be a cynic, because he
alone is supposed to know the future. But tell
me," she added, her eyes brightening with
mischievous inquiry, "why is it that you, my
own countryman, are the only one of the quar-
tette who has not been to see me? Your
friends, Messieurs Deschanteaux, Petroffski, and
the accommodating Don Calvo have called
several times and paid the penalty for it with
numerous games of cribbage, for my aunt is
merciless. Are you afraid of cribbage?"

He shook his head, and a smile crept into his
eyes. Her presence was warming him into
life.

"I would brave even that to see you," he
answered with mock gallantry; "but," he

added, "those who would fill their cask with
bubbling, joyous life must joust right merrily,
and my armor is rusty and my sword
blunted."

"Wherefore?"

"I met the black knight Disappointment in
the lists and he unhorsed me.   By the way,"
he added, for he was impatient to switch the
train of conversation from the siding of himself, where it threatened to run into a swamp,
to the main line of generalities, which was
smooth and had no end, "have you ever been
upon the tower?"

She craned her full white neck, looking up-
ward.

"No.   One must have a beautiful view."

"Would you not like to go up there?   We
can sit there and chat if you have the time."

"I am not Time's slave, but he waits upon
me.   I never sacrifice my liberty of action nor
of impulse to Time nor to Mrs. Grundy.
Allons."

He pulled the rope that hung from above the little wooden door that led to the spiral staircase. It opened, and they ascended, she first, lest her foot slip on the uneven stairs; he there to catch her, wishing a slip. Half way up they passed the guardian, and Forrest dropped silver into the itching palm. They emerged upon the platform, out of breath, for the strongest lungs pant after short effort, at this height above the sea.

She gazed, speechless for a time, at the white-topped volcanoes, the broad plain of Anahuac, the placid shimmering lakes, and then down at the broad Plaza, where men were as ants moving. "The impression is exquisite," she said at last, when she had caught breath and speech, "but weak. It lacks character, strength, ruggedness. There is no incentive to action in it all. The Hindoo Buddha on the lotus flower, chained eternally to contemplation, would be more fitting here than Thor with his hammer. Perhaps, after all, it's a question of atmospheric pressure."

He nodded approvingly. "Climate, soil, and aspect of nature mould the races," he said.

"But not the individual," she interrupted quickly. "We can break through the hard crusts of heredity and environment, and challenge the laws and powers of nature to combat. Call it spirit, self, what you will, there is the kingdom of the microcosm, in which the 'I' is overlord."

She was looking, as she spoke, at the snowy cone of Popocatepetl, as if addressing it, as well as the man who leaned over the railing beside her. He looked at her curiously, with a sense he knew not whether of disappointment or rebellion. Most men instinctively hate intellectuality in women. Their ideal, au fonds, is the harem. For all of which men are not so much to blame, for in climbing the heights of brain development, women of our land usually leave sex and flesh in the valley, only the skeletons reaching the peak, there to grin at each other in a charnel-house.

His glance fell upon the book she held in her

hand and he read the title.   It was *Dulce y Sabrosa!*

"You are reading my favorite novel, I see," he said.

"Yes," she replied, "and because it is your favorite novel. I overheard what you said to Monsieur Petroffski about it in the Alameda, for you remember I was seated just behind you. I determined to get the book if possible, curious to know what the ideal woman of such a man as you might be."

In her slight emphasis of "man" there was Carlylian contempt of mostly fools ; her distinction of him was flattering to his pride.

"And what do you think of Cristeta ?"

"Delicious and unique.   I can readily see how real men worship such women.   From time to time women have given all for love of men, but they are few.   When one does, and the love is returned, I think a star falls into the diadem of God."

He looked at her again, this time with a

strange feeling that defied analysis. He yearned to know whence came this woman. He questioned tentatively : " You speak French and Spanish so well, you must have lived long in Europe ?" Trite but effective.

She divined his thought. "I am an enigma to you, n'est-ce pas ? I am to most people, though I rarely give the answer. I will tell you all about myself you would care to know." She settled herself down comfortably upon the broad stone bench, her elbow on the railing, her head resting upon her hand, and started as one drawing a full breath for a long run.

"I feel like a chronicler. To begin. I was born in Pennsylvania. My father was a German miner, uneducated, a Hercules in strength, good-natured and loving, who worked his eight-hours' shift in the coal-pit, and thought life worth living. He married the sister of a fellow miner, a Hungarian. She was a sweet-faced woman with soft, pleading eyes. I can see her now, though perhaps the mist of years has dimmed the

sharper outlines. We lived in a little two-
roomed hut that was not always fast against
wind and rain. When my father came home
and had washed and eaten, he would take me
upon his knee and tell me the story of Prince
Charming. How the Prince came at last, after
weary, wasted years of waiting, to the maiden
who loved him. He was always mounted upon
a handsome charger and clad in all manner of
glittering array. It was the only story my father
knew, and I never tired of hearing it. There was
always the same suspense, doubt, and pain,
flavored to some sweetness, though, by the delicious foreknowledge that it was to end well.
My father lacked the imagination to change the
facts of the story; he could only change the costume of the Prince and the color of his horse.
Sometimes he came clad in silver armor, with
mantelet of emerald green; in gold and purple; in
steel and blue; now mounted upon a black
charger, again upon one milk-white; but always
with bag of gold at saddlebow, from which he

flung largesse. Poor little father! It was the only gold he ever saw. It was a puzzle to my childish mind why there should be such lengthy discussion as to the possibility of my having a new pair of shoes when Prince Charming was scattering largesse à deux mains."

There was nothing in this tale of a childish tale to make a mist float before the eyes of the man listening. Perhaps something in the tone of the soft, musical voice, that broke, once or twice, under the weight of memory, moved him more deeply than he would have cared to own. He sat beside her, keenly intent, one leg crossed over the other, his hands clasped about his knee. They were alone in the tower, and the city seemed to have sunk farther away.

Feeling a sympathy, in the Greek sense of the word, she took up the thread and went bravely on. "I remember well it was my high ambition at that time to own a pair of shoes and, more than all else, long stockings that would come clear up to my hips, partly because they would be so beautiful, I thought, and partly to protect my bare legs from scratch of brier and thorn-bush. But that longing was never gratified. When I was eight years old my father was killed, crushed by a falling mass of rock. When they brought him home the neighbors gathered around, offering help to lay out the dead, but my mother waved them away and barred them out. She then knelt by the body, putting one arm about the neck of him she had loved in life, bringing her face close to his. She crooned and whispered to him, and as the night fell fast, I became afraid, and crept from the corner, in which I had crouched, to the bed. The starlight came softly through the window, soon to be blotted out, for black clouds were banking up, winged by the north wind. Feeling, I found one of his hands, ah, so cold, and one of hers, warmer, and I knelt there clasping a hand of each in each of mine, my head resting upon the bed. My mother's crooning and whispering grew lower, and I think I must have slept or fallen into a stupor. I dreamed that the room

was filled with an intensely yellow light, and
that my father, dim and indistinct in form and
face, but with eyes that were clear and had a
glory in them I have never seen in human eyes,
took me by the hand. He told me again the
story of Prince Charming, not in words, but as
if in a series of visions, in the last of which I saw
the Prince, dressed in blue, and his face was a
very human one, never to be forgotten. Then I
saw my mother's eyes beside my father. They
wavered a moment and were gone. The yellow
light went out too, and I awoke just as the white
dawn was creeping in. My mother lay with her
head upon my father's breast. The room was
intensely cold. During the night fine snow,
driven by the wind, had sifted in through the
cracks and crannies of the cabin and covered the
bed and those who were upon it as with a thin
white pall. My mother's hand was cold too.
She was dead."

She had said these last words very softly, her
voice sinking to a whisper. The man roused

himself, unclasped his hands from his knee, and taking one of hers, pressed it gently.   Her musical tones had lulled him into a dream wherein he had *seen* the things she told of, as visions rising and floating by, conjured by melody.   It did not surprise him that she should tell her heart-secrets to one she had scarce met before, for he well knew that affinity is a link that time does not forge, but which is moulded with the swiftness of the electric spark, upon mere contact, and one feels that it is but the physical counterpart of a chain that has been for ages.

"Well, after that," she continued, with new strength in her voice, and as if opening a chapter with less pathos, "a good woman took me in for a couple of years and herded me kindly with her own brood.   One day there came to our village a troop of acrobats, and the manager happened to notice me, and asked to have me join him.   He would teach me.   It was at the time of a great strike, and bread was scarce, so I went, and for years lived a strange life with people who were not cruel to me. I learned to perform on the trapeze, to sing and to dance. I have known what it is to tighten my belt, on going to bed, to still the cries of hunger. And yet, after all, it was not a bad life. When I was sixteen I had wandered over the greater part of Europe and our own country. Men flocked about me, offering gold and what not, and I would have yielded time and again, perhaps partly from desire of change, partly from the cravings of sex, but every time there came to me the story of Prince Charming as told by my father, and I said to myself, it is not he ; some day he will come and will find me true and waiting. Then a brother of my father, who had been a professor in Leipsic, sought me out. Through the death of a relative he had come into possession of a small fortune, which enabled him to realize the dream of his life, which was to travel and meet men great in science, whom he had before known only by correspondence. After that I lived and travelled with him until his death, which oc-

curred last year.   And so endeth the chroni-
cle."

She had galloped through the latter part of her
story, impatient to have it over, feeling it was
too long and lacked climax.

Her companion had resumed his former position, with his hands clasped about his knee.   He
was not looking at her, but his face was turned
three quarters toward her.   She studied his features for a moment, and then a thought seemed
to flash upon her.   She grew pale to the lips,
and put her hand to her left breast as if she
would compress the beating of her heart.   The
emotion passed quickly away, and then there
came into her eyes a look of infinite gladness.

He was thinking of this woman beside him,
born in a hovel, long classed as one of the
world's outcasts, steering her life-bark with a
fairy tale, the tiller gripped by an iron hand,
though.

The thought broke in upon his musing that it
was his turn to tell of himself.   He rambled on

to her, a tale trite enough, bare of outer things startling (so it seemed to him, though she listened, wide-eyed).

They talked on till the shadows fell, and the dark-faced, wrinkled guardian peered out upon them from the door which led to the stairway, wondering what two could do in a tower, thus long.

The man and woman descended and walked together across the great square. On the southerly side of it, where her car passed, she turned and put out her hand.

"Good-by until tomorrow only," she said. "I will expect you at my aunt's at eight. There will be quite a crowd there, but you shall not play cribbage. We will find time for a chat. Adios."

"Yes, I will surely be there."

He pressed her hand, helping her at the same time to mount the step of the waiting car. As it moved off she turned and bowed to him again from the platform. He lifted his hat, and then walked up the Plateros toward the Concordia, where it was his custom to dine on a chop or steak, a tortilla of black frijoles, and a pint of Pyrenean wine.

Jornada III

The Villa Dominguez, Tacubaya,—first road to the right after you pass the gambling hall,—was alight and ablaze.

A square two-storied house with stuccoed walls, set in the middle of an acre of palmettoes and cacti, with here and there a gigantic nogal, giving shade grateful at noonday. Here and there a plaster statue gleamed white against the dark green background of leaves patched with fragments of dark blue sky. For this night lamplets, glasses filled with oil in which floated a burning wick, had been placed among the branches and in the centre of huge century plants, glimmering like weak fireflies.

Carriages and hacks drove up to the arched

gateway, and many men and some few women emerged therefrom and walked up the gravelled path to the glaring doorway. In the drawing-room, hideous with a set of American furniture which sprawled over a crimson carpet that was like unto a pool of blood, Madame Schreiber received her guests with subdued enthusiasm and much mixture of tongues, Don Calvo beside her, master of introductions.

"Señora Schreiber, my friend Pepe Taluno ; La Señora Schreiber, Pepito."

They swarmed in, these youthful Mexicans, each having loaned Don Calvo y Ramirez a considerable sum for this invitation and introduction, the fame of the niece having spread far and wide. Such a harvest had the accommodating gentleman never dreamed of, and his popularity had waxed with his purse.

Madame Schreiber had never dared to hope for such social eminence, and looked upon Don Calvo with favor; and Alma Lessing herself, though aware of his weaknesses, smiled upon

him with the indulgence of one whom something neither pleases nor bores. She cared little for the adulation of which she was the
object, but her aunt's enjoyment was so un-
bounded and childishly frank, that her niece
had not the heart to thwart the good lady's
plans for forming a salon in Tacubaya after the
manner of celebrated women about whom she
had read.

Some things move more rapidly in Mexico than
in other lands, and within a week Alma had
had a half dozen offers of marriage, and one
of love and affection—the latter from Deschanteaux, one of the former from Petroffski. While
she refused the Russian, she had kept his
friendship and a dog-like devotion that was
boundless; the Frenchman had ground his teeth
and permitted himself to say some brutal things
under the lash of her sarcasm. She was not
offended that he had asked her to be his mistress, for like many women of strong passions
and intellectual development, she cared little

whether a ceremony tied her to the man she loved. She had felt, for opportunity for judging from actions had been lacking, that his character was as small as his stature, and she had sped her shaft at the fatuous presumption and insolent assurance which were as twin pedestals to the man's words. It had bitten deep, this shaft, and the wound yet rankled within him, but he had plastered it over with a laugh, and continued to call at the Villa Dominguez, received good-naturedly. Unquestionably in love with her, as he had never been before with womankind, he had a faint hope in a long siege, and in the meantime he would make it unpleasant for any man to whom she might show favor, a curious balm for the wound of unrequited love which men of Gallic race have indulged in from time to time before the worms have eaten them.

This night Deschanteaux sat beside Alma upon the straight-backed, uncomfortable sofa, a challenge in his half-closed eyes and thin-lipped

mouth for every one of the black-coated men
who formed a solid half circle about this fair
woman. Among these were Mexicans, a Frenchman or two, a German count who had accepted
the one alternative of peddling life insurance
policies for a living, the other one being star-
vation ; an Englishman who had travelled and
had not forgotten it; an American author celebrated for writing proper and pretty things that
were as crisp pie to every good household in
the land. The conversation twisted from Spanish
into French, dropping now and then into English, for the celebrated traveller had never really
thrown off the shackles of Ollendorf, while the
pleasant author pretended to no language but his
own.

A few tables were about the room, at one of
which old General Bisbee, the senior of the
American colony, was deeply engaged in a game
of cribbage in company with his son-in-law and
a red lady in green. In another corner were two
women, the one tall, angular, bare-armed, and

décolletée, undeniably homely, and equally thoroughbred ; the other small, plump, with pink and white complexion, and hair that was the color of new hemp. The former was the wife of an English gentleman who had heavily invested some one else's money in a rich gold mine, and had gone West to examine into the matter, leaving his wife stranded in Mexico to kill time as best she might ; the latter was helpmeet to a Protestant missionary, a good man from Ohio, who had striven bravely many years to make a convert from among these heathen.

"Lady Mackelroy," said the plump one to her companion, casting a timid look toward the corner where Alma sat, "do you think she is —a—perfectly respectable ?"

"Who? Alma Lessing? Quite so. Did you think she was a tart, Mrs. Sommers ?" and Lady Mackelroy let fall her fan of black ostrich feathers upon her knee and gazed at the little woman with indulgent curiosity.

"A—a—what?" ventured Mrs. Sommers.

"Oh! I said a tart."

"And may I ask what that is?"

"Certainly. It is the latest London slang for a woman who has divorced most of the thirty-nine articles, and who lives half according to the dictates of nature, and half according to the bank accounts of her admirers. One can't really define a slang term, you know; one must feel it. No," added Lady Mackelroy, after a moment's pause, during which the little woman was studying out this definition, "Alma Lessing is quite good form, I fancy. I heard of her in London last season, though I did not meet her there, and she visited some very good people. What made you think she was—how did you put it?—not respectable?"

"Oh, nothing," said Mrs. Sommers, meekly. "Only she dresses so curiously and is so—so *easy* in her manners."

The English woman raised her lorgnette to her eyes, and after studying Mrs. Sommers for a moment, "My dear Mrs. Sommers," she said, "that is a Greek gown somewhat modified, a costume not one woman in a thousand can wear with grace. I admit that her total lack of jewelry is immodest, and as for the way she attracts men, *that* is simply criminal."

"Yes, indeed," replied Mrs. Sommers, with approving emphasis. Lady Mackelroy heaved a little sigh, hid her face for a moment behind the black ostrich feathers, to conceal either a yawn or a smile, and then glanced toward the doorway. There she spied a man who had just come in, and, after looking around for the hostess and failing to find her, was leaning against the wall, with folded arms, seemingly bored.

Lady Mackelroy whispered to Mrs. Sommers, "Who is that man over there by the door? He looks like a sleepy lion."

"That is Mr. Forrest, a New Yorker, a mining engineer. He has been quite unfortunate. He is real nice."

"Ugh!" muttered Lady Mackelroy to herself;

" the idea of calling a man of that size ' real nice.' "

Forrest knew that Alma Lessing was behind the semi-circle of black-coats which he saw at the other end of the room.   To attempt to approach her would be awkward, so he preferred to remain where he was until she should see him.   His patience was not tried, for Alma, remembering his promise, was alert to his incoming.   For much thinking of him she had scarce heard the English traveller's description of Borneo; did not smile when he said, with great impressiveness, " Les habitants sont des cannibaux qui mangent la viande humaine;" and a tale of weird adventure in the craters in the breasts of the great Ixtaccihuatl, told by a tragic-looking Mexican, had failed to interest her.   More than one had noticed that she was distraite.

"Will you excuse me, gentlemen?   There is a compatriot of mine over there whom I wish to speak to."   She rose, and they moved their chairs hastily to make way for her.

When she had passed beyond them Deschanteaux turned fiercely to Petroffski. "I thought
you told me Forrest had never called here," he
whispered.

The Russian shrugged his big shoulders. "I
did not know he had seen her since that Saturday on the Alameda; but we do not own her,
mon cher, and it is no business of ours whom
she sees."

"I'll make it my business," muttered Deschanteaux; and then, after a moment's observation,
he added, "She is going out, evidently for a
walk in the garden ; suppose we play écarté
until she comes back. Holà, Escandor, will you
take a hand at écarté ? "

Unimpressionable as he was in his present
listless mood, Forrest could not but be struck by
the beauty of the woman who advanced toward
him. She was clad in a white drapery, sleeveless, and wore not a single jewel of any kind,
more for the reason that she had none than from
any affectation of simplicity. She would cheer-

fully have worn a queen's diadem, but only the tawdry would have been within the reach of her purse. She passed her hand under Forrest's arm. "Let us walk outside a while," she said; "I am suffocating in here. You were good to come."

"Glad to come, you mean," he replied. "I am late ; but this by reason of the breakdown of my car. I was compelled to walk the greater part of the way."

They went out into the garden, full of green blades and glimmering lamplets that warned of the sharp points. By a plaster statue of Diana Huntress, accompanied by the usual impossible dog, was an iron bench.

"Let us sit here a while," she said; "how deliciously cool the air is, almost sharp ! Perhaps the wind is blowing from the white mounds of Ixtaccihuatl."

He threw himself upon the bench beside her.

" I'm afraid I've left a dozen or two enemies in the room," he said, with a careless laugh. " You seem to be obsédée to-night."

"It's the usual thing," she answered, quietly, "and I assure you I do not enjoy it particularly. I am what is called a man's woman, and I suppose they like to talk to me, or at me, or for me, as the case may be. Sometimes I think *ils se pavanent*. There was no one there to-night who interested me, excepting Petroffski, whom I like. Your friend Calvo is une bonne bête, and I am not sorry to be of service to him in lining his coffers. As for Deschanteaux, I despise him." She said these last words without any shade of anger in her tone, as she would have spoken of the weather.

Forrest condensed his interrogation and interest into one word, "Deschanteaux?"

She caught the key and hedged a little, for his sake, for it was more in her character to strike where she would. "Is he a good friend of yours?"

"I scarcely know. I have known him since he was a child of six, and am rather fond of him. We were at the Lycée together. I was an orphan and without friends. His mother was kind to me." He glanced up at the four posts of Pacari Tambo, and as if this contemplation of bright stars induced Aurelian meditation, he continued aloud : "Friendship is a peculiar thing. It can hardly be said to exist to-day as it did in Greece or Rome or even in the middle ages. It is now but a cobweb chain at best, and money or woman may cleave it as Saladin's cimeter did the silk handkerchief."

His tone aroused her sympathy. "You like him. I should not have spoken as I did. But, believe me, his nature is incapable of friendship as of love. He is to me a pretty, petulant child, malicious to an incredible degree. I only say this because something tells me he is more your enemy than your friend."

"I fear he has offended you," replied Forrest.

"No," she said, with a light laugh, "it is I who have offended him. It is difficult to offend me. I care too little for others, as a rule, to be moved by their opinions or the expression of them. He amused me a while. Now he bores me."

They were silent for a time. The moon had risen and was throwing its silver sheen over the white Diana and the impossible dog, the bayonets of the palmettoes and the curved leaves of the cacti ; the lamplets dimming to yellow specks in these white rays. The soft strains of *Sobre las Olas*, played by the excellent band in the gardens of the gambling-hall, rolled through the still air toward them, full and sonorous. Forrest felt as if the sound rippled the moonlight into waves, he floating thereon, into the Nirvana of nothing, whither he had listed so much of late. It was dimly strange to him that he should be so unmoved beside the one woman who was so like unto the ideal he had wrought out in idle hours. He had a vague feeling that he ought to care for her; that any one else would think it quite extraordinary that he did not; but caring for anything was altogether too much exertion anyway. He wished he had some life, strength, passion, energy, wondering dumbly whither they had all gone. Easier to float than think, after all; to sway on the waves of light and sound.

She could but marvel at what manner of man this was, this listless giant. Surely she had recognized the face she had seen in her vision in the hut years ago; yet this was not the way the prince should have come to claim her. Dreams are but half true at best. She had divined from what he had told her of himself in the tower how the fire of energy had been quenched under disappointment, until there scarce remained a glowing ember; but this she would fan into flame, she would sting him into action, rouse within him the strength she believed but slumbered.

His mood of silence was contagious. She too stared at the moon, blankly. This orb was now to her as a crystal ball of the Rosicrucians, whereon she saw pictures of the past and future, these latter formed by hope. Yet was she aware

that there was a current between them, an ebb
and flow of the sub-conscious, building deep and
strong and lasting, to which words would have
been but as the chatter of apes to the undersong
of the sea.

How long they sat thus she knew not, for she
had ceased to hear the dull tread of time, and
was seeing the moon now trebled through a tear,
when her aunt's voice called loud and sharp :

"Alma, Almita, donde estas? Come in. We
are going to have a game of cribbage with the
General."

She felt as one who, dreaming upon a flowered
bank, has rolled off into a ditch.   Forrest started,
shame-faced, stung into movement by the feeling that he was a loathsome thing. With a
swift motion he took her hand and kissed it.
"I think I am a ruined man, Alma.   Of all those
in that room," and he pointed to the lamp-
flaming windows, "there is none so worthless
as I."

She stood fronting him in the white light, the

most glorious figure of a woman he had ever
seen, and in her eyes was an expression any
man but himself would have read, and then
thanked God for life. She would not speak the
words that rose to her lips. If he could not
feel what she would say it had better be left
unsaid, for the nonce. She put her hand on
his arm and they strolled back to the house.
At the door he stood aside to let her pass.

Deschanteaux sat at a table, holding some
cards in his hand, and when Forrest and Alma
Lessing entered he looked up at them and the
corners of his thin lips drew down into a sneer.
"Tiens," he said to his companion in a tone
that could be heard throughout the room,
designating Forrest with a backward movement of his hand : "Monsieur has evidently
been enjoying himself in the moonlight. Il a
l'air d'un coq en pâte." His voice was a jeer;
it cut like a saw into the flesh. The others
knew it meant an insult, deep and incurable,
levelled at both the man and the woman. It

rang the death-knell, probably, of one of these two men, in a land where nought but blood can polish anew a tarnished shield.

Every eye was fixed on the tall American. There was upon his face seemingly neither annoyance nor anger. He walked slowly and carelessly toward Deschanteaux, and there was suspicion of drawl in his tone as, stopping at the table whereat the Frenchman sat, he said, very quietly: "You forget where you are, Paul. Your remarks are in exceedingly bad taste."

He then turned away and crossed the room to where Alma stood leaning against the back of a chair. "Good night," he said, and then added in a lower tone: "I am sorry to have brought this upon you. You see I am always in bad luck. I think I had better go away now to avoid any more unpleasant scenes. I know his character. He is not fully responsible for all he says."

"Good night." She pressed his hand, and

for a moment her features relaxed again into the look she had given him in the garden.

When Forrest had taken leave of Madame Schreiber, now trembling like a leaf in a breeze, and muttering under her breath an endless series of "Ach! Gott im Himmels!" and the door had closed behind him, Alma Lessing walked over to Deschanteaux and stood facing him, her bare arms folded. He rose from his seat as she came toward him, the same jeering mask upon his face. The woman towered several inches above the man. Her eyes glittered with suppressed anger, but her voice was cold and hard, though the effort to keep it so was perceptible. "Monsieur Deschanteaux," she said, "this is the second time you have insulted me in my own house. I am not une grande dame, as you know, but a plain woman of the people, and from childhood have been compelled to defend myself, and I have never given any one else the right to defend me. I have tolerated your presence here and

overlooked your petulance as I would that of a
boy. Now, Monsieur Deschanteaux, will you
leave this house of your own accord, or put me
to the unpleasant task of picking you up and
throwing you out?" She spoke in French,
clearly and distinctly; and all present, watching
breathlessly this bit of tragic comedy, could
see the muscles of her round white arms swell
and the two red classic bows of her lips press
tightly together, her whole form quivering for
physical action. They well knew that for a good
part of her life she had trusted to the strength
of those arms for a living, and there was not a
man there who did not believe her able to carry
out that which she threatened. She was of the
stamp of those Teutonic women of old, great
white bodies crowned with hair of reddish
gold, defending broken camp with spear and
arrow against short sword and round buckler,
women upon whose white breasts warriors
slept, passion-tired—so thought the American
author to whom now and then came ideas he

did not insert in his home and fireside series, for his name guaranteed ignorance to innocence.

So perfect was the conviction that this woman could take care of herself that not even Petroff-ski, who worshipped the ground touched by her slippered foot, moved from his seat to her assistance. Deschanteaux did the only thing possible under the circumstances. He bowed in silence and walked out.

"He'll kill that big American," said the English traveller to General Bisbee.

"If he can," chuckled the General.

It was getting late, and soon most of the guests came forward to take leave of the two women. Alma was quiet and easy, as if nothing worth remembering had occurred, but her aunt was prey to conflicting emotions. She saw her prospective salon ruined by this contretemps. "C'est bien dommage," she said to every one ; and every one said, "Ah, oui," without quite knowing to what part of it all she alluded.

"Don't you think it rather—ah—forward of

her, Lady Mackelroy ?" queried Mrs. Sommers, tentatively, as these two adjusted their cloaks in the ante-room.

"Oh, certainly !" replied her ladyship, knotting a white hood under her chin ; "the proper thing, if anything, would have been for her to have screamed or wept, or to have gracefully swooned away in close proximity to the best-looking man in the room. How tickled poor Sir John would have been to have witnessed this."

When Forrest left the Villa Dominguez he walked to the terminus of the tramway and perceived a car just coming in, which meant that it would not leave again city-ward for half an hour. He was undecided whether he would not walk, but, concluding to ride, entered the car and sat down in one corner. A few moments later he heard voices, and some of the guests of Madame Schreiber, in company with Don Calvo, all talking at once, came into the car. In the dim light of the smoky oil lamp Forrest was not recognized by the newcomers, for his dress suit was covered by a gray over-coat, his slouch hat drawn down over his eyes.

"Oigame Vd.," said Don Calvo, excitedly shaking his finger at one of his companions, "I tell you his conduct was unpardonable. Had he been justified in any grudge against Don Jorge he should have waited until some other time and place."

"Que mujer! hombre!" wedged in Escandor, rolling a cigarette, "did anyone ever see such a goddess!"

"Moralles told me that Deschanteaux said, as he got into his carriage, that he would kill Señor Forrest before forty-eight hours, though the American will stand more provocation than any man living."

"Yes, yes," interjected a short, dark boy, eager to tell what he knew. "Listen, Señores. You remember the duel between José Latour and Hidalgo some two months ago? Bueno. The next day I was at the baths, and Don Jorge Forrest was in the steamroom, and we were talking of this, and he said that in his part of America duels were never fought, and that the practice was silly and childish."

"Bah!" replied Escandor, "he must fight. These American ideas don't go here. Not a man nor a woman in Mexico would ever speak to him again. He must fight or leave town by the next train."

"He is no coward, of that you may rest assured, Señores. He will fight him." Thus Don Calvo, always loyal to his friends.

"Caramba!" said a tall, thin Mexican who had not hitherto spoken, "who would not fight for such a woman? He would have to be lower than a dog. Give me the chance and I would fight the whole French colony of Mexico."

"He could crush him in one hand"—"a bullet is no respecter of size"—"the larger the man the larger the bull's eye"—"he is a good swordsman, Deschanteaux, quick as a snake to strike," etc.

So they rattled on till the car, which had

started, stopped before the entrance to the gardens of the gambling-hall, where a great number of people were waiting. As they crowded into the rear door, some finding seats, others standing, Forrest slipped out of the front and started on foot for his lodgings.

He was anxious to escape them, these men who judged without knowledge. "He must fight" rang in his ears. But they did not know what this man was to him, he whom he must fight. He strode along with quick, nervous pace, leaping now and then over the form of a drunken indio sprawling on the narrow pavement. Passing along the edge of the Alameda, he turned into a street on the right, and hammered with his fist upon the huge door of an old house. The sleepy portera opened, rubbing her eyes, and he passed into the patio and then up the stairs to the gallery whereon was the modest room he occupied. It was poorly furnished. An iron bed; a table loaded with books and papers ; clothing, spurs, saddle, and boxing gloves hung upon wooden pegs driven in the walls, from which the plaster had fallen here and there. A shabby piece of carpet half covered the red brick floor.

He took off his coat, and then threw himself upon his bed to think it all out, and of much thinking there was sore need. Now he had at least a few hours of quiet to settle with himself ; with others later. Matters with him had now come to a climax ; this climax the bottom of a gulf down which he had been stumbling many a year. Bad luck had stalked him like a doppelgänger, and had now brought him to bay. To see things clearly one must go back, tracing cause and effect down the steps of time.

He saw himself at the age of twelve at a lycée in Paris, orphaned, dependent upon an uncle, a good-natured man who gave cheerfully and with open hand. Deschanteaux had been his friend, two years younger, of much less stature and strength. A malicious boy, he remembered him, given to hysterical fits of crying and screaming when things did not go to suit him, continually appealing to le grand American (and successfully) when other lads threatened merited thrashings. Madame Deschanteaux, learning from her son that George Forrest was his friend and protector, used to take them both out on Sundays to dine at the café, and then for a drive in the Bois, or a trip to Isigny, where the Deschanteaux owned a farm, though Paul's mother lived at Rouen. Friendless as Forrest was in that great city, these were his only outings, and he was grateful to the good woman for her kindness. She, leaving them at the gate Sunday evening, each with a huge package of bonbons to be eaten thereafter by stealth, would say to Forrest, "You will take care of Paul, Georges, and see that he does not get hurt?" and he had always promised, saying simply, "Oui, madame, bien sûr," and he was not one of those who forget things promised.

Later these two had gone apart. Forrest,

shaking off the leading strings of school, had taken a room in the Latin Quarter, and entered l'École Polytechnique. Paul had gone to the University, and pulling through, tant bien que mal, had entered the bureaucracy, department of diplomacy, aiming at St. Petersburg. They had met now and then on Sunday excursions. In Paul the man had kept some of the traits of the child. He was subject to fits of colère froide, as the French call it, a cold rage that may wear itself out in time, but does not re-act into the warmth of good fellowship. None better than Forrest knew his weakness, and often held the hands of the younger boy while he made vain efforts to scratch and bite him. In Mexico they had met again, and it was to Forrest like a breath from the springtime of youth. Only a month before this he had re-ceived a letter from Paul's mother, rejoicing that her son had met his old comrade, and end-ing with the old-time request, "You will take care of Paul, Georges?" And now he was asked to kill him or be killed by him, *au choix*, or else flee like a thief in the night, branded. No other way out of it, turn it how he would. Leave he could not, for he had not the money to pay his way out of the country, had he been so inclined.

He was not over fond of existence, anyway. When he left college his good uncle had left life, cheerfully and good-naturedly, as he had lived, and, furthermore, had left a will wherein, with much legal rhetoric, he had constituted George Forrest his sole heir and legatee, and creditors would have smacked their lips at the reading thereof. Unfortunately for Forrest the will was the only part of the estate which had been found, the kindly man having genially scattered his wealth to whistling winds, and his fortune had ended with his own need of it. The young man had come home, a stranger in his own land, and pushed his way to the swine's trough, hunger-driven, and illy did he succeed at it. Some men drop into this century by mistake. Either they

were intended for another, and there was some
blunder in time, or they do carry with them such
strong marks of past incarnations that they fit into
this one no more than square pegs into round
holes. Imagine a Cœur-de-lion awakening in a
broker's office, holding his nose to the stench of
ghettos which have burst bonds and swarmed
the world over, making good shield of promis-
sory note 'gainst lance-thrust, with heeling bail-
iffs, writ-armed, nosing for chattels. His was a
misfortune common to those of his countrymen
who have passed much of their youth in older
lands. His own was to him filled with clamor
and confusion and all manner of din. Accus-
tomed to yield deference to intellect and genius,
he found it exacted by politicians and pork-
packers, and his stomach would not feed on that
meat, hard though he tried to gulp it down. He
had been born with the most fatal of all gifts,
that of seeing things as they are. Luck had been
against him too, and repeated misfortune had
wearied him into a condition of lethargy in

which he cared not whether the world turned or stood still.

At last a chance had come to him to manage a mine in Mexico, but unfortunately the property belonged to honest and inexperienced men who had capitalized it at an honest valuation and attempted to raise the money on an honest business basis, whereupon the brokers had laughed them to scorn, and the owners deservedly and miserably failed, leaving their manager penniless in a strange land. It seemed to Forrest that fate had done its worst when there came up this matter of killing his friend or getting killed by him. He did not so much mind the leaving of a world for which he had no love, but, if this must be, preferred to choose the manner of his exit.

And Alma ? Paul evidently loved her much to make him thus lose his head and fling even ordinary courtesy to the winds, when she but walked and talked with another man ; though Forrest did not know that when Alma Lessing had reëntered the room with him, her expression and manner were as an open book to the keen eye of jealousy, and Deschanteaux had clearly seen that the game was up for him.

As for Forrest, ah, how he could have loved this woman had not some strange wall, he knew not how, built itself about him, penning in every impulse, every desire—or was it that impulse and desire were drugged into a dull sleep by environment? Nothing more painful and brain-racking than self-analysis. He felt dimly now that some subtle action was within, a tremor in a chrysalis; but perchance the morrow would bring counsel, so he slept.

Jornada IV

THERE were few in the great blue-tiled Venetian palace that was the home of the Jockey Club at the early hour of eleven in the morning. In the cardroom some devoted ones were gathered together for a game of alburres; on one side of the large salon an Englishman was writing letters, while upon the other the great General Roca, he of Queretaro fame, a stout man with red face and bristling white moustache, was asprawl upon a sofa, studying the smoke wreaths of his cigar. In a huge, leather-covered chair by one of the balconied windows Paul Deschanteaux sat reading, or pretending to read, a yellow-backed novel, with now and then a nervous yawn.

He knew that Forrest, having no occupation, was wont to pass much of his time in this club, lounging, smoking, and looking over the papers, and the Frenchman was hot to meet him again, fearing lest in some way the American escape him. His purpose was more fixed, if possible, than it had been the night before. The occurrence at the Villa Dominguez had not given birth to hatred as hail from a blue sky. Rather was it that envy, worm-like, had long since eaten out the heart of friendship till there remained but a thin shell, which at slight pressure

16

would burst like a puff-ball. He had suffered from childhood the humiliation of protection, and had resented it. Exile and ennui had soured him. He longed to break the monotone of wearying days ; and then the woman's words, too, had bitten like corrosive acid, and now he dared look no man in the face till he had settled with this favored one who should do battle for her. All this had keyed him up to bursting. He hoped to meet the American here, and even at this moment the hand of the man he sought was laid upon his shoulder.

"Paul," began Forrest, who had come up unheard, "can we not talk this matter over? We have been friends for too many years to quarrel now, and——" but Deschanteaux bounded from his chair and faced him, livid. "I do not accept your apologies," he shrieked in a voice that was heard throughout the building. "I told the men last night that you were a coward, and I repeat it now: un lâche, un grand lâche, hiding behind the petticoats of your mistress! A beggar and a coward!" He raised his right hand to strike the American in the face, but Forrest seized his wrist in a grip like that of a steel vise, and twisted it till he threw the smaller man, grimacing with pain, back into his chair.

The card players in the adjoining room had rushed to the wide door and were watching curiously, knowing something of the reason of this dispute, for gossip had borne high upon its tide the events of the preceding night at the Villa Dominguez. General Roca, however, sprang to his feet with an agility younger and slimmer men might have envied, and ran to Forrest. "Let go of his hand," he said, sternly; "I will see that he does not try to use it. We must not settle disputes here á bofetadas, as between two peons in a back alley."

Forrest did as he was bidden, and Deschanteaux sank back into the chair.

"You are witness, General," exclaimed Deschanteaux, "that this man came here to apologize, and that I refused to accept his apologies. I——"

"Brrrrmm!" interrupted the General, clearing his throat with a rumbling roar, his small, black eyes snapping with excitement; "I know what I know. I take charge of this matter now, and both of you must obey me. Do you go home, Monsieur Deschanteaux, and find two friends. Don Jorge, stay a moment, I wish to speak with you."

Deschanteaux arose, and with a jeering laugh: "I depend upon you, General, to see that he does not escape." He left the club, followed by two of his friends, to whom he held forth, down the stairway and across the broad patio.

General Roca liked Forrest, and, on the other hand, had not forgotten the matter of Maximilian and his hatred of the nation which had backed this unfortunate prince. He spoke the language only under protest, snorting at the mention of things French, and declining to wear silk hats made in Paris.

"Don Jorge," said the General, turning to Forrest, "do you entrust your interests to my hands? Yes? Brrrmm—then go to your room and remain there till I come. Adios."

He patted the American gently toward the hallway, and then, turning back, rubbed his hands briskly together. "Unfortunate affair, gentlemen, very unfortunate!" he exclaimed to those who stood discussing the matter. "I hope you will say nothing of this until it is over. On your honors, gentlemen, for you know the police are sometimes disagreeable. Brrrmm!"

He was in his element, was General Roca. Two things in the world he loved and lived for. To tell the real truth concerning the siege of Queretaro to any who would listen (and of late these were few), and to be mixed up in a duel, either as principal or second. He was in great demand in the latter capacity, as he almost invariably got the best of everything for the one for whom he acted, including luck in the result.

At two o'clock the General arrived at Forrest's

room, accompanied by his nephew, Pepe Ximenez, a young cavalry officer with soft, dark eyes, and cheeks that were red as ripe peaches.

"We had a time, amigo mio," exclaimed the General, sinking into a chair, "with his seconds ! Two Frenchmen, caray, who pretended to give me lessons, and they have yet to grow beards ! They were sucking milk when I was leading cavalry ! They claimed their principal was the offended party and had the choice of weapons ! Dios ! I put them straight in one—two—three. They held out for pistols, claiming that you were so large and strong. 'Diablo!' said I, 'your friend should have thought of this before offending mine.' Brrrmm ! So swords it is, hombre, till one falls, to-morrow morning at five, at the Military School building, the usual place, out there by the Peñon."

He chuckled with satisfaction, wiping his face with a huge red handkerchief, and then continued : "And how are you at the sword ? Good, I hope."

It struck Forrest that the General should have made his ability as a swordsman the subject of inquiry before consenting to these weapons, but it had sufficed for Deschanteaux' seconds to want one thing for the General to want another—and get it. He replied, however, that at one time he had known something of fencing, but for years had not had a sword in hand.

The General glanced inquiringly around the room. "You have no foils? Pepito, hijo mio, go to my house and ask your aunt Teresa for my foils and masks. Tell her it is not I who fight, and you will save her several hours of prayer in the church of St. Joseph." When Pepe had departed, the General turned to Forrest, explanatory: "We will practise a while and get your hand in again. By the way, this matter between you and this Frenchman reminds me of an episode that occurred at the siege of Queretaro. Brrrmm! You see the armies were this way—" He illustrated on the table. "This inkstand is Queretaro, this button the convent of La Cruz. General Escobedo and his staff are this book. I and Velez were thrown forward here with two battalions. Naranjo and Guadarrama commanding the cavalry are this cigar."

Forrest followed the movements intelligently, expressing interest, criticising, winning the old man's heart. "You understand these things, Don Jorge mio," the old soldier exclaimed with enthusiasm. "You should have been a soldier— a leader of cavalry—a Murat! Dios! What a picture you would make, charging at the head of a troop of horse! En avant! Sabres flashing, bugle braying—tra—la—la—la. Brrrmm!"

Here Pepito entered, the foils concealed under his military cloak, which he carried on his arm, the masks wrapped in a newspaper, looking like a huge melon.

The General stripped off his coat and waistcoat, took off his collar, and turned back his shirtsleeves, adjusted the mask, and commanded Forrest to do likewise.

"Pepito, push the bed back, and that chair out of the way—the table in the corner—so. En garde now ! Bueno. Let us begin at the beginning." The blades clicked. The General continued, voluble. "Your left foot more at right angle. So. One, two. Parade. Quicker, hombre ! A woman could run you through with a bodkin. That is better. Now swords quarte and watch this flanconnade. Bad, very bad. Parade in octavo, so and so. Let us try it again. Quicker, I tell you. Carramba !"

The General lowered his sword. "Don Jorge," he said, solemnly, "I hope you will not disgrace me by going to sleep on the ground to-morrow morning. By the Mother of God, put more life into your movements, mas vida, hombre! You have the strength of a Hercules, and are slower than a burro. You should be able to bind my blade and whip it out of my hand with a demi-turn of your wrist. Imagine I am Deschanteaux, and am about to carry off the beautiful Señorita you two are quarrelling about. Try it again. En garde ! "

This time it was better. A slight flush had passed over the pale face of Forrest at the mention of the woman. The General chuckled, knowing he had struck true. " Better, much better. Now thrust. Quarto, tercio, circulo. Better and better. Attack ! Dégager ! Feint ! One, two. Brrrmm ! "

The General took off his mask. " Now, Pepito, take a turn with Señor Forrest."

The young man seized the foil, and for another half hour he and Forrest fenced, the General seated in the bentwood rocking-chair, a cane in hand, playing at maître d'armes.

"Good, Don Jorge ! Are you a cripple, Pepe ? That time he had you, chiquito. That should have been quinto, not tertio. You had a good teacher, Don Jorge, that is evident. Mark this: if you are in doubt as to a parade, do nothing. Keep your point directed to your adversary's nose, and, as your reach is longer, he cannot touch you without first spitting himself like a chicken and spoiling his beauty. Ha, ha, ha! Brrrmm! That reminds me—at the siege of Queretaro—no, now I think of it, Pepito, teach him the Indian feint. Attention, Don Jorge! One, two. There, you were fairly touched and a dead man without the buttons, and you can't see how it was done. Slowly now, Pepito, so he can get it."

The two combatants, out of breath, sat down upon the bed. The General glanced at his watch. "Five o'clock. I have an engagement to keep, and will return at seven. We will have another hour's practice. You will dine lightly. A small piece of chicken, a bit of bread, and one glass of champagne, nothing more. To-morrow morning a roll, a cup of coffee at four, and at four fifteen the carriage will be here. I leave nothing to chance. Were it not for this habit of mine, at the siege of Queretaro—well, well, I will tell you that later. Adios!"

He bustled out, after a hand-clasp, followed by Pepito, and Forrest was alone.

He lit a cigar and sat down in the rocking-chair. No help for it now. What a demon Paul was, after all! Surely he, Forrest, had done all he could. They were both now in the hands of fate. There is always a relief in shifting things on to the broad shoulders of destiny. In olden times they called it "the judgment of God," and presumably there were some who believed that. The chances, so far as Forrest knew, were even. If he fell, the leaving of his life would become him about as well as the living of it. Neither was a matter of consequence. He remembered that under these circumstances men wrote letters and made wills, facing the worst. He had no one to whom he cared to write and nothing to leave. Did Alma care much for him? Did he care for her? Something like a sharp pain shot through him at this thought. He wished he could see her once more before to-morrow morning, to tell her—no, better not, better for her and for him. But the wall about him was crumbling, the mist was fading away, and he saw clearly.

It was only last night they sat in the moonbeams, by the white statue of Diana and the impossible dog, and it seemed years ago. What a droll life this is, after all!

Alma Lessing, parched for news, had sent posthaste for Don Calvo. Her action of the preceeding night was wormwood in her mouth, and to undo it she would have given much. Well had she said it, ''a plain woman of the people.'' Arms akimbo! The polish of later years cracked now and then to let out nature; the lioness growled from under the sheepskin. But this would have been to her no more than the breezes that blow, did she not know that the man she loved would pay the piper for her dancing. Snakes are dangerous to monarchs, and to her Deschanteaux was a coiled adder, ambushed. Custom would demand ten paces and two bullets, senseless leaden things with no more respect for the heart of Hercules than the ribs of a guinea-pig, or a clashing of steel blades with open spaces for

even weak hands. Without her outburst matters
might have been smoothed over, the break in
years of friendship mended, to last at least for a
while.

It was not in her nature to lose time in regrets.
The night through she had writhed, impotent,
under conjured possibilities, but the sun smote
her into action. She penned a hasty note to
Don Calvo, having full faith in his devotion.
Would he not watch, inquire, spy out, letting
her know results, and this quickly, to the
foundering of horses?

She paced the room till after the noon hour,
when he arrived, breathless and bursting. He
chaptered the events of the morning at the
Jockey Club, while she beat a nervous tattoo
upon the arm of her chair. He was verbose
to weariness, and her impatience whipped him
on. The town was now chewing details of
the matter, for each witness had whispered
them to a friend in solemn confidence. The
two would fight—that was settled, then—but

when and how? Don Calvo swore he would tell her before nightfall, and sped away, shaking with sympathetic excitement.

The task was not an easy one, for principals and seconds were mute. Don Calvo buttonholed General Roca in the San Francisco, insinuated questions, and was laughed away. Later Don Calvo laughed, for he straightway sought out a big brown fellow in a peaked straw hat and ragged cotton shirt, and, after earnest whispering, slipped silver into his hand, betaking himself thence to a café to kill time with a game of dominoes and await the return of his ferret. He waited long, for the carriages were already rumbling back from afternoon drives on the Paseo when the man returned, his sloe-black eyes glistening success.

He had lured the coachman of General Roca to a neighboring pulqueria, and there, after pouring down him many glasses of the milky· fluid, had learned that the horses were not to be taken out that afternoon for the usual family ride to

Chapultepec, but were to be hitched up at four the next morning ; and Manuela, the housemaid, had seen the General furbishing his swords, the pair he kept in the long table drawer in his library. This was enough for Don Calvo, and he was off to report.

He found Alma quiet without, but quivering within. There is relief in knowing the worst. To-morrow morning at five or so—swords—of course within the walls of the roofless and unfinished building of the Military School. Every one goes there to settle these matters. (Ah! yes; she remembered how Forrest had pointed it out to her that day in the tower, a reddish blot on the plain.)

She plied him with questions. Was the Frenchman skilled at sword play ? Was Forrest ? As a rule how many were killed and how many wounded in these encounters ? She calculated chances, but the best gave her a twinge of pain. She dreaded his lethargy; she feared good nature, remembrances of past friendship, would numb his arm and bridle his impetus, while she knew the other would seek to kill. Her lover was to her as some big child whom she would have folded in her arms, shielding him with her body, could she have done so. Her lover? He had never spoken to her of love. She had seen him twice—three times at most. To her he was the prince coming after weary years of waiting; but what was she to him? Yet she felt no doubts upon this score; in this she was sure of the future. Only now he risked his life; the prince's horse might stumble upon the very threshold and throw its rider; and this must be looked to.

Yet she could do nothing. There was no act by which she could prevent this encounter upon the morrow. Too much had been done already. She could not disgrace him further. She had dragged out of Don Calvo the words of Deschanteaux: "Coward, hiding behind the petticoats of your mistress!" The word "coward" to him stung her to madness;

17

the reflection upon her was nothing. No, he
must fight ; fight and win and kill. She was
merciless as Judith, and could have slain with
her own hand ; but she was powerless.

Nay, she could do something. She believed
in the triumph of will over destiny; that thought
creates and fashions events to one's liking if
one be strong enough. Her uncle had taken
her much among men whose names were
towers in the higher world of knowledge, and
she had heard them whisper of science reaching out an arm into the domain of miracle and
wresting fixed laws from the chaos of superstition. The power of one mind upon another
had been dimly seen, and men were wondering
if some musty records of past ages could be true.
It seemed to her that she could radiate a strength
that could stop a star. Love would ride the
warhorse of her will to battle. She had a faith
to move mountains. From her room, on the
morrow, she would move these two fighting
men as puppets. She felt like a witch mixing a

mystic brew, to save to her the man she loved ; and while this man slept, heavily, dreamlessly, the woman watched in her darkened room, her eyes fixed upon vacancy, her mind intent on what was to be, till her body became rigid and motionless, and her thought, taking form, sped like an electric shaft to mould events to her liking.

Jornada V

The carriage rattled over the stony streets at the first glimmer of the dawn that was paling the lanterns. of watchmen at street crossings. On the rear seat were Forrest and the General, opposite to them Pepe Ximenez and Doctor Lisorta, the latter fighting yawns. Forrest was thinking nothing of whither he was going. He had awakened with the vague feeling of an incubus pressing upon him, of some ugly task to be faced and done, and when the facts shot back into his consciousness he had put them away, convinced that thought of them was useless—an hour or two would tell. He sat looking out of the carriage window at the long gray line of houses, dotted here and there by the gaudy signs of dramshops, scarce heeding the animated dispute which had arisen between the General and the Doctor.

At the turning of a street corner Forrest gave a slight start, for he saw, under the sharp light of an electric lamp, a form clothed in a white, trailing garment, and the face, though indistinct, he knew to be that of Alma Lessing. She seemed to glide to the carriage door, and then sweep along beside the vehicle, without an effort, so close that he could have put out his hand and touched the long brown hair that fell like a cloak to her feet. He recognized at once that this was but an hallucination, a thought picture thrown out objectively, yet it caused a curious tremor to run through him. So strong was this impression, so persistent, that he turned to the other occupants of the carriage, almost in wonder that they too should not see. When he again looked toward the window, the phantom of his brain had vanished.

The carriage had passed the limits of the city, and, stony roads left behind, was now bowling over smooth earth, the horses snorting in the keen air, the coachman restraining them with oft repeated "Xo, xo, chicos."

The General and the Doctor continued their argument. "I tell you, General," said the latter, shaking his finger, "the French lead the world in scientific investigation, and to-day we are entering upon the era of science."

The General shrugged his shoulders and waved his hand contemptuously. The Doctor continued, emphasizing by slapping his knee, "Man, from that period of evolution in which he assumed his present form, has passed through three stages, and is about entering the fourth." He counted on his fingers. "First, the period of brute force, the age of the warrior. Secondly, the period of cunning, the age of the priest, who, by shrewdness, overcame brute force in a measure, and gathered to himself the functions of legislation, leechcraft, and monopolized all knowledge. Thirdly, the period of law, based upon experience and observation of human relations, the age of the lawyer, who holds us in his grip to-day. We are at the dawn of the fourth period, during which the scientist will rule, and the practical scientist is the physician. He only can save life; the others destroy it."

"The period of pills, in short," interrupted the General, grinning maliciously.

The Doctor threw himself back upon the cushions, folding his arms, and raising both shoulders nearly to his ears, a method of expressing indignation which was too deep for words. Pepe Ximenez laughed.

"War," said the General, in more serious tone, and shaking his finger triumphantly in turn at the Doctor, "is acknowledged by all historians to have been the great civilizer. Hence the soldier is the prime factor in civilization."

The Doctor sniffed. "The soldier's greatest virtue is courage. It is also possessed in an equal degree by numerous animals, such as the rhinoceros, the crocodile, the shark——"

"Disparates ! All the great qualities——"

Here the carriage stopped, and the black peaked hat of the coachman, with its silver band, shadowed the window. "Is it here, Señor General, you wished to stop ?"

The General thrust his head out and surveyed the surrounding country. "Yes, yes."

He opened the door and they alighted. When all were out, the General sent the carriage on to take a stand some half-mile up the road, that attention might not be attracted, for one can see far on this treeless plain.

The four walked in single file along a narrow path worn through the grass, and which led toward the huge brick walls pierced with holes which some day, government funds permitting, were to be closed into doors and glazed into windows. As they were about to enter under an arch, Forrest again saw the white form, more dimly than before, floating like a bit of mist over the grass, and it seemed to melt away against the brick wall.

At the other end of the enclosure stood three gentlemen in black frock coats and silk hats, conversing together. The General glanced at his watch and said, with an air of relief, "We are not late. In fact it lacks five minutes of the hour."

The sun had now fully risen and was sending broad bands of light through the window-spaces, checkering the hard earthen floor into squares of yellow, framed in dark brown.

The Doctor went over to a low pile of brick, and after carefully depositing his black bag at his feet, sat down and began rolling a cigarette, like a veteran actor who, having no part in the first act, awaits his cue in the second, indifferent. Two of the black frock coats advanced to meet the General and his nephew, saluting gravely, the manner and expression of polished gentlemen, with a smacking of undertakers simulating sympathy.   The seconds of Deschanteaux were both of his own country.   Monsieur Imbert, an amiable youth with blond moustache, much out of place in a matter of this kind, would have given worlds to be back in his glove store in the Coliseo, in company with the charming woman who kept his accounts. That morning she had said to him when he left her, "Courage, mon pauvre chéri," and he had shrugged his shoulders in contempt of feminine alarms.   He kept repeating to himself, however, that he was only a second, a mere spectator, and hence in no possible danger.   He relied upon his companion for all things pertaining to this business, and well he might, for Gustave Delorme was a man of wide experience in killing with or without deliberation, strictly according to social law and usage.   He had served in the Chasseurs d'Afrique, knew a sword from a curling iron, and felt the honor and responsibility of his position, which reflected in the measured gravity of his speech and the curving gesture with which he twirled his pointed black moustache. He had great admiration for General Roca, whom he had described to the peaceful Imbert, " Voilà, mon cher, un vieux de la vieille, un vrai ! "

Monsieur Delorme proffered a pair of swords, his own. The General examined the handles and guards critically, tried the spring of the blades over his knee, measured them carefully side by side, and then accepted them—they were full four ounces heavier than those he had brought with him, and he preferred the weightier blade for the stronger arm. The details were again agreed upon, and the General walked over to where Forrest stood, gazing at nothing, his thoughts filled with the woman whose phantom he had seen, a great yearning within him.

" All right, my boy," said the General, cheerfully, "the conditions are that you fight till one falls, as I told you yesterday. A wound that does not disable will not warrant interference by the seconds. Don't forget what I told you about the length of your reach. Above all things, wake up! Be quick!"

Forrest bowed in acquiescence, and took off his coat and waistcoat, laying them upon the brick pile upon which the Doctor was seated. He rolled up his right shirtsleeve to the shoulder, displaying a massive and muscular arm, white as a woman's, at which the Doctor glanced in admiration.

Forrest took the sword which was handed to him, saluted, and stood facing Deschanteaux. The blades clicked together, and the two men looked into each other's eyes. The corners of the Frenchman's mouth drawn back, and his eyes half closed, as if to concentrate his power of vision, gave to his face an expression wherein one could read fixed determination, intense vindictiveness, and certainty of success. His gesture in bringing his sword to that of his opponent spoke the satisfaction of one who has waited long and says "At last."

For a moment Forrest saw only the friend

of boyhood days. Remove the moustache, smooth out the lines about the eyes, and he was again, "le petit Paul, sacré garnement, vas !" of twenty years before. Forrest felt an almost overpowering desire to throw down his sword, seize the hands of his adversary and hold them, while the latter tried to bite and scratch, scream-ing the while. He had always been so careful not to hurt him, hearing the words of Madame Deschanteaux, and remembering his answer : " Bien sûr, Madame;" and his mouth recalled the sweet flavors of bonbons, eaten by stealth, lest the pion see them. Only for a moment did these thought-pictures flash through his mind; but his eyes showed absence, and the point of Paul's sword quivered within an inch of his side.

The General uttered a terrible " Brrrmm !" at which Monsieur Delorme looked indignant, but he could say nothing; for when a man is troubled with catarrh, he must clear his throat once in a while.

Forrest understood. He gripped the handle of

his sword more firmly, recalling that latterly life had become worth living, worth fighting for. The gloomy future had been pierced by a ray of light. All remembrance of past friendship fell from him now like a cloak thrown off, never to be worn again. He kept his eyes fixed upon those of his adversary, seeking to guess his thrusts, acting upon the defensive. There was a scratching of steel upon steel, with now and then a low, sharp click.

It was rapidly becoming apparent to the onlookers that Deschanteaux was master of the art; as superior to Forrest as cat to mouse. Deschanteaux' expression was now a triumphant grin; he knew he had the other at his mercy. It was easy, almost too easy; so a glance said which he shot at his seconds. He was now playing to the gallery; he would keep this up as long as it amused him, and then with one swift thrust—in the right spot.

The General nervously grasped the arm of his nephew, who stood beside him. He felt that he had blundered, blundered horribly in the choice of weapons.   With pistols his principal would have had at least a chance; here he had none. The General saw that Forrest was not "asleep," as he had feared ; he saw that his man was doing all that he could, better than he had done the previous day in practice ; but even this was nothing.

Forrest felt his own lack of skill, knew now that Deschanteaux would do with him what he would.   There was no fear in him, only regret, deep, poignant, and it condensed itself into one word, "Alma !"   It was almost as if he had uttered this name aloud.   The illusion came to him again; the white-draped form was beside him, so close he could have touched the long, brown hair; so clearly defined that it was passing strange the others could not see it.   A puff of cold air seemed to blow upon him; a tremor waved up from his feet to his head, and through his arms.   Then a flame leapt within him, and a rosy cloud, as of mist tinged with blood, passed before his eyes, through which he saw only the grinning face and the neck of Deschanteaux, swaying like a pendulum from side to side.   He felt the strength of an army in his arm. The Berserker rage was upon him; he could have shouted, as his Viking ancestors had shouted at sea, perched upon the prows of their long boats, driving into the face of the storm with clashing bucklers.   He was not conscious of his own sword ; his hand moved itself as move upon the keyboard the fingers of a skilled player who is thinking of other things.

General Roca marked with amazement the sudden change.   He saw the lips of Forrest part, showing the white teeth clinched together ; the angry flash in the eyes, and two deep, perpendicular lines in the centre of his forehead.   Now Forrest attacked.   His sword play had ceased to be fencing, it was legerdemain.   His blade had become invisible, moving so swiftly the eye could not follow it, a moulinet forming a shield of steel.   He moved upon his adversary slowly, deliberately.

Deschanteaux broke ground. A step back, then another. When he put out his sword it was whirled aside like the switch a child thrusts into the spokes of an engine wheel in motion. His expression changed ; at first doubtful, troubled, finally one of absolute terror. His eyes were fixed, as if fascinated, upon the disk of steel before him or upon something beyond. His arm was numbed, his hand had lost its dexterity. Back, step by step, with now and then a weak thrust in vain attempt to break through.

The spirits of General Roca rose. He cast upon Monsieur Delorme a look that meant much. The Doctor left his seat and came nearer. This could not last long.

Suddenly Forrest's arm straightened, he bent forward very slightly, then the hand and sword were still, only the end of the blade quivering a little, and it had changed color to red. At the base of Deschanteaux' neck, just above the breast bone, a stream of dark blood gushed out, and at the same instant his knees doubled up under him, and he fell heavily upon his back.

Monsieur Delorme sprang toward the fallen man, but the Doctor was there before him. Sinking upon one knee, he turned the body half over, and at the back of the neck saw a small wound from which issued a few drops of blood.

"He is dead, gentlemen," he said quietly, looking up at the anxious faces ; "the sword passed completely through the neck, severing the cervical vertebræ. Death—or at least the cessation of all consciousness—was instantaneous. He suffered no pain."

Monsieur Imbert grew very white, and went over to the pile of bricks and sat down, hiding his face in his hands. General Roca turned to Monsieur Delorme :

"This is unfortunate, sir, very unfortunate ; but you recognize, of course, that all conditions have been strictly complied with, and that this is a catastrophe which we deplore as much as you do."

18

Monsieur Delorme nodded affirmatively. " Yes, yes, General," he replied sadly, "it is the fortune of war. I will sign the procès-verbal together with my companion, if you will draw it up."

George Forrest glanced at the body of the man whom he had believed to be his friend for so many years, and then, throwing down his sword, turned away and walked over to where he had left his coat.

He felt neither sorrow nor triumph. Something of the anger which had so strangely and suddenly arisen within him was still upon him. He had thought it all out before to weariness, and knew that he had done what he could to avoid the meeting ; his reason justified him and dominated his emotions. Then, too, a change had taken place. The mental inertia, amounting almost to a form of melancholia, had fallen away from him. The blood coursed rapidly through his veins and tingled in his finger-tips ; every faculty and desire alive, vibrating in unison with the nature that was about him. The sunlight was bright, the sky blue, as to him they had not been for many a year. One chapter of his life had closed, tragically, it is true, but another had opened in which he could foresee rainbow tints flashing about a woman's face, and her voice was the music to which the hours stepped lightly.

" You know, Jorge," said the General, coming up to him, "you will have to keep out of the way for a few weeks. The police will make no great effort to arrest you, but if they should see you, they could hardly avoid doing so, for form's sake ; and once in Belem prison, it is not easy to get out, except feet foremost, the typhus aiding. We will make our report, Monsieur Delorme and I, later on. Now I will drive back quickly to your house with you, and, while you are packing a few things, will have the horses changed, and send you the carriage with a fresh pair which will take you out to the third station on the railroad, where you can get the train."

The General signalled to his coachman, and

he and Forrest entered the carriage, leaving the Doctor and Pepe Ximenez to assist Monsieur Delorme in the sad task of bringing back to the city the body of Paul Deschanteaux.

They had proceeded only a short distance when the General's ear caught the sound of horse's hoofs, a mad gallop upon the highway. In another moment the panting animal was reined up by the side of the carriage and the face of Don Calvo appeared at the window. He espied Forrest.

"You are not hurt, Don Jorge mio? No? May the saints be praised! And the other?"

The General answered with a look, a shrug, and an outward motion of the hands that told the story without words. Don Calvo's good-natured face grew serious; he commented with a word, "Ca-ray!" uttered slowly and softly, straightened up in his saddle, and removed his hat, riding along a few moments in silence. He leaned over again.

"Don Jorge, I am glad you are safe, and another will be more glad than I can tell you. I have two letters for you which I was only to deliver in case you were unhurt." He handed the white envelopes to Forrest. "I am going back to carry the news to—" He hesitated, and then, perceiving that Forrest understood, continued, "I promised her, you know. Adios." He waved his hand in leave-taking, and, putting spurs to his horse, shot along the highway, and was soon out of sight, swallowed up by a cloud of white dust.

"Read your letters, my boy, read your letters," said the General, patting his companion on the knee; "I'll warrant they contain good news."

Forrest opened the smaller envelope. The enclosure contained but a few lines, which he read at a glance. "If you read this, fortune has favored you and you will know that I am glad beyond words. Come to me as quickly as you can. Alma Lessing."

He folded the note and put it in his pocket.

He did not need this to confirm the certainty which was within him, yet it caused his heart to beat faster for a moment, added another glow and a brighter hue to rainbow tints that played about the face filling the future.

The other letter enfolded some bank bills, and was from his friend Velasco, the notary. "I give this to our mutual friend Don Calvo, who tells me he will see you early to-morrow. My sympathies are all with you, my dear friend, and likewise the good wishes of my comrades. Now if you are unscathed I have good news for you. Don Cassio Alvarez—you know, the one in Guerrero—has authorized me to close with you for the management of his hacienda. I take your acceptance for granted, and send herewith some money for travelling expenses, for which please send receipt—on stamped paper—at your convenience. He is a good man, Don Cassio, and a pleasant companion, well educated, and I know you will like him. Enclosed find full directions for journey. Afsmo amigo y S. S. Q. S. M. B."

Forrest handed the letter to the General, who read it carefully through. "Good!" he exclaimed, seizing Forrest's hand and shaking it heartily. "It is great good fortune that this comes now. And I know Don Cassio well. He is one of the old ones—was with me at Queretaro. I must send him a letter by you. He will confirm all I told you about the siege; he is a bright man, a bright man, a very bright man."

Surely the jade fortune had turned her face toward him, smiling, so Forrest thought, and her eyes were two wells of deep blue, fathomless. He wondered if—now that—

The carriage drew up before the house in which Forrest lived. "I will not see you again for a long time, perhaps, Don Jorge." The General seized Forrest's hand and passed his own left arm about his companion's neck, patting him on the back, Mexican fashion. "You have nothing to reproach yourself with, my friend. You have acted in all things like a brave man and a caballero. You were over-matched, and how you did it in the end is a puzzle to me. However, thank God you are sound and well! Go with God, hijo mio, vaya Vd. con Dios!"

The General waved aside the thanks which Forrest would have uttered. "Nada, nada! I came too near putting my foot in it in choosing swords. Only that last attack of yours—carramba, what an assault!—saved me from disgrace." He leaned out of the window, beaming, as the carriage turned, and called out again to Forrest: "José will be back in half an hour, remember, with fresh horses."

Forrest rapidly thrust some clothing into a large valise, together with his revolvers and things that were trifles in a city, but beyond price in the wild country whither he was bound. The rest of his luggage Velasco would send on to him. He wrote a note to the worthy notary, thanking him warmly, explaining why he could not call, and gave this to the portera, with some silver, for delivery later.

He sprang into the waiting carriage after flinging the words at the driver : "First, José, the Villa Dominguez—Tacubaya—first road to the right after you pass the gambling hall."

"Si, Señor."

As the vehicle rumbled off, Forrest drew up the blinds, as a measure of precaution, while passing through the city. He could take no risks now. The fast trot of the horses was a snail's pace to his impatience, and every now and then he glanced out, through a crack, astonished at so little progress on the way. Time was to him now like a bit of rubber, that one could stretch out, stretch out, indefinitely. Thoughts of the new chapter, almost formless, but hinting at bright things, hummed through his brain.

At last. José drew up the horses and Forrest had passed under the arched gateway, and to the door of the Villa Dominguez, which was wide open. He stood for a moment, uncertain whether he should ring, and then heard her voice from within, bidding him enter.

Alma Lessing, clad in the gray dress she had

worn the first time he had seen her in the Alameda, was reclining on a couch at the farther end of the great bare parlor, by a window. She beckoned him to take a seat upon a low stool beside her, and as he did so he took her extended hand in both of his.

Now that he was in her presence the confidence he had felt was shaking ; it might be only a dream born of his wish—perhaps the whole scaffolding he had built up was the work of his own imagination—to vanish like mist before the stern objective facts of reality. He began awkwardly, some trouble showing, perhaps, in his face.

"You know?" he asked.

"Yes," she answered ; "Don Calvo was here an hour ago. He told me what I wished to know."

She read him like an open book printed in clear type, and her heart bounded within her. Oh, he of little faith ! Oh the great, big, blind, stupid, blundering child ! She smiled mischievously. She would prolong this torture for a moment to punish him for doubting woman's love—compensation to follow.

"It was strange," he said, reflectively, "I don't know how it happened. He was a hundred times more skilful than I. He had me at his mercy until—" He felt reluctant to go on ; it appeared somewhat foolish to him now—at least when expressed to others—to her, perhaps— and these illusions of his had something sacred about them to him. After a moment's hesitation he plunged on : " You may think it curious, but the fact is there was a moment I thought you were beside me. I could see you as clearly as I see you now, and then I fought like a mad man." He grew reckless ; she could think him a fool if she would. "I saw you more than once while we were going to the place. You seemed to be with me all the time. I suppose I was very nervous underneath, though I did not know it."

Still she said nothing. The little mischievous smile had faded from her face.

He crossed his legs, clasping his knee in both of his hands, his favorite attitude. His hopes were dimming and the silence oppressed him ; he felt he must break it.

"Well," he said, his eyes fixed on the red carpet, "you see, I have got to go away. General Roca told me I must keep out of the way until the matter had blown over. I had a letter from a friend of mine this morning, offering me the position of manager of a hacienda out in Guerrero. It is not a bad place. Dull and lonely, and all that, I suppose, but plenty of work. General Roca has loaned me his carriage, and I am to catch the train at the third station out, some ten miles from here." His voice had the note of weariness in it as of old, and the woman could bear it no longer.

She laid her hand on his and sought his eyes, compelling him to look at her, to read in her face the truth, and then—doubt was laid aside forever. There came to him the full comprehension of her love—of a love that recked not of the world, that was without bound or limit, such as falls to the lot of man once in ages ; and, as he bent down to her, she whispered:

"May I go with you ?"

With a cry that was almost a sob he fell upon his knees, and wound his arms about her till he lifted her from the couch, she yielding to him gladly, in the fulness of her self-surrender. As their lips met he knew that his thirst for her would never be quenched, though their lives were to span beyond those of mortals, and she believed that another star had fallen into the diadem of God.

www.ingramcontent.com/pod-product-compliance
Lightning Source LLC
Chambersburg PA
CBHW020121070726
47497CB00021B/1709